DECADES

Fleetwood Mac

Mac

in the 1980s

Don Klees

sonicbondpublishing.com

Sonicbond Publishing Limited
www.sonicbondpublishing.co.uk
Email: info@sonicbondpublishing.co.uk

First Published in the United Kingdom 2023
First Published in the United States 2023

British Library Cataloguing in Publication Data:
A Catalogue record for this book is available from the British Library

Typeset in ITC Garamond & ITC Avant Garde
Printed and bound in England

Graphic design and typesetting: Full Moon Media

Acknowledgements

Thank you to Stephen Lambe for the opportunity to write again for Sonicbond. I also remain exceedingly grateful to everyone who's challenged and encouraged my writing over the years, not just this book but also in general. In that respect, I particularly want to spotlight Al Cattabiani. In its own way, his invitation to contribute to CultureSonar in 2015 played as big a part in me writing this book as all those years listening to Fleetwood Mac's records.

Likewise, I'm thankful to family and friends alike for being both encouraging of and patient with me (and this book) over the past year. Foremost among this group are Beth, George, Patrick and Will, who make my life richer in far too many ways to account for here.

Would you like to write for Sonicbond Publishing?

At Sonicbond Publishing we are always on the look-out for authors, particularly for our two main series:

On Track. Mixing fact with in depth analysis, the On Track series examines the work of a particular musical artist or group. All genres are considered from easy listening and jazz to 60s soul to 90s pop, via rock and metal.

On Screen. This series looks at the world of film and television. Subjects considered include directors, actors and writers, as well as entire television and film series. As with the On Track series, we balance fact with analysis.

While professional writing experience would, of course, be an advantage the most important qualification is to have real enthusiasm and knowledge of your subject. First-time authors are welcomed, but the ability to write well in English is essential.

Sonicbond Publishing has distribution throughout Europe and North America, and all books are also published in E-book form. Authors will be paid a royalty based on sales of their book.

Further details are available from www.sonicbondpublishing.co.uk. To contact us, complete the contact form there or email info@sonicbondpublishing.co.uk

Follow us on social media:
Twitter: https://twitter.com/SonicbondP
Instagram: https://www.instagram.com/sonicbondpublishing_/
Facebook: https://www.facebook.com/SonicbondPublishing/

Linktree QR code:

DECADES | Fleetwood Mac in the 1980s

Contents

Above: Despite recording some of their best music together, Fleetwood Mac's members spent the 1980s mostly walking separate paths.

Below: The band had a new line-up by the decade's end, one that was more cohesive but also less exciting.

Introduction

In a history spanning more than 55 years, there have been over a dozen different Fleetwood Mac lineups. But for much of the general public, only one of them truly matters. During their time together, the combination of Mick Fleetwood, John McVie, Christine McVie, Stevie Nicks and Lindsey Buckingham created music that balanced art and commerce like few others before or since. The popularity of this quintet's first album together – the 1975 release simply titled *Fleetwood Mac* – might've seemed like an overnight success to those who didn't know the band's backstory, but in reality stemmed from years of relentless effort, both individually and together.

Foremost among their success stories was the 1977 album *Rumours*. Written and recorded as multiple relationships within the band were collapsing, the landmark album became a worldwide hit that still attracts new fans. Disbanding would've been a rational (and healthy) response to the turmoil that surrounded making the record, but a collective passion for the group and the music they made together, dictated a different path. The quintet continued touring and recording even as tensions continued to accumulate, both within the group and externally. Stevie Nicks explained in a 1981 interview: 'I've seen people get the wrong impression of five people I love, because it doesn't work every time, especially if you're so confident that it *will* work.' Despite her mystical image, Nicks – who'd emerged as Fleetwood Mac's breakout star – was remarkably pragmatic. 'It's truly better to stay at number 2, because there will always be the hope of doing something more creative and better. When you're number 1, everything goes to the wind, and there's no place to go except down.'

Fleetwood Mac only released two studio albums in the 1980s, but four of the five members released solo records during this period. Though these varied in terms of artistry and popular acclaim, each succeeded in bringing the members' individual contributions to the band into focus. Of their albums together, the deliberate emphasis on traditional pop-craft over experimentation on 1982's *Mirage* was well-received commercially, but left some band members feeling ambivalent about future collaboration. A few years later, individual circumstances converged to overcome that reticence, resulting in *Tango In The Night*: an album closer to the mark artistically and commercially. Lindsey Buckingham told *New York Times* music critic Stephen Holden in 1987: 'When the group left the road after the *Mirage* tour, there were many issues left unresolved.

This album is as much about healing our relationships as *Rumours* was about dissension and pain within the group.' Despite the talk of healing relationships, Buckingham left the group rather than go on the road again.

The conflicting accounts of Buckingham's 1987 departure are a reminder that any telling of Fleetwood Mac's story needs to make allowances for a multitude of perspectives. A combination of personal agendas, substance abuse and the nature of memory itself *ensures* that; however sincere any given recollection might be, some sit uncomfortably next to documented facts. If this sometimes makes the band's history seem like the love-child of Akira Kurosawa's cinematic examination of subjectivity, Rashomon and a prime-time soap opera, it at least offers one of the most engaging soundtracks of the rock era.

As the *Rumours* incarnation of the band splintered from the late-1980s into the early-1990s, it took a request from a US President to fix it, if only temporarily. The band's one-off performance for Bill Clinton's 1993 inauguration came between two less-successful Fleetwood Mac albums. Each featured a different lineup – the latter of which even Mick Fleetwood conceded was one too many. He declared in 2001: 'It was a good band, but the one major misjudgment in terms of carrying on.'

A gradual mending of fences – especially a musical *détente* between Buckingham and Nicks – led to a fully-fledged reunion in 1997, and set the stage for further drama. The continuing tension between the band members' individual and group efforts – embodying the truth that this quintet worked best *together*, but could only do so for limited periods – reinforces how even more than the 1970s, the 1980s were the band's pivotal decade. Likewise, with the drastic lineup changes – many driven by irreconcilable differences – Fleetwood Mac was the quintessential band for the era in which divorce was no longer taboo and blended families became more the norm. As much as the band exemplified most of the quintessential elements of rock-star drama, the Fleetwood Mac story remains uniquely compelling.

Prologue: World Turning

When discussing Fleetwood Mac in the 1980s, the five musicians who first came together in 1975 and made some of the era's most enduring pop music, all share roughly equal significance. But when considering the group's origins, the most influential figure might be an individual who neither belonged to the band nor ever had any official affiliation with them. Fleetwood Mac would not have existed in any form if not for British blues musician John Mayall.

Much as actors are often said to be no more than six degrees of separation from leading-man-turned-character-actor Kevin Bacon, Mayall was a major nexus in the British rock scene. In the 1960s, his band, The Bluesbreakers, included numerous musicians who went on to further international success. While this led to repeated lineup changes, in the long run, it also added considerably to Mayall's prestige.

Eric Clapton and Mick Taylor are just two of the many players for whom The Bluesbreakers provided an early showcase, but Mayall's ear for talent wasn't limited to guitarists. Various members of his rhythm section also had wide-ranging careers after leaving the group – including bassist Andy Fraser who formed the band Free, and drummer Aynsley Dunbar whose later work ran the artistic gamut from Frank Zappa to Journey. Mayall alumnus drummer Colin Allen later toured with Bob Dylan and co-wrote songs recorded by bands, including Wings, and a group founded by former Bluesbreaker Michael John Kells Fleetwood: better known as Mick Fleetwood.

Born in Cornwall in 1947, Mick Fleetwood spent a large part of his childhood in Egypt and Norway, where his father was stationed as an RAF pilot. Not a terribly studious young man, Fleetwood was fortunate to have parents who recognized and encouraged their childrens' artistic leanings. His oldest sister Sally attended art school, while his other sister Susan trained at RADA and played numerous film and television roles before her untimely death in 1995. The parents bought their son a drum kit when he was 13 and ultimately supported his decision to leave school and move to London to pursue a career in music.

He soon met keyboard player Peter Bardens and joined his band, The Cheynes. After a period of earnest effort as an opening act and a trio of unsuccessful singles, The Cheynes disbanded when Bardens joined Van Morrison's band Them. Bardens had remained friendly with Fleetwood, and after leaving Them, invited the drummer to join his new band Peter

B's Looners in 1966. The lineup included guitarist Peter Green who left later that year to join Mayall in The Bluesbreakers, having previously performed with them as a short-term substitute for Eric Clapton.

By this point, the band had morphed into Shotgun Express, featuring Rod Stewart as one of their singers. Fleetwood stayed with the group until they disbanded in February 1967, and in April, Peter Green contacted him about joining The Bluesbreakers. Though the drummer's tenure with Mayall was brief, it nevertheless turned out to be significant by virtue of introducing him to one of the most important people in his life: bassist John McVie. Slightly older than Fleetwood, John McVie had been with The Bluesbreakers since 1963. Born in London's Ealing neighborhood in 1945, he started playing music in earnest in his early-teens. Like many of his friends, McVie started out on guitar, but soon switched to bass (in the mold of Jet Harris from Cliff Richard's backing band The Shadows) and joined a local band called The Krewsaders.

Despite his interest and aptitude for music, when McVie left school in 1962, his plan was to become a civil servant. Because his training to become a tax inspector overlapped with John Mayall assembling his own band after several years as a sideman, for a time, it looked like McVie might do both. When a fellow musician recommended him to Mayall, the bassist jumped at the opportunity, but opted to keep the day job. In an online Q&A in 2004, McVie recalled that his first day at the tax office was also the day of his first gig with The Bluesbreakers.

After nine months of office work during the day and gigs at night, McVie decided to focus on music full-time. That could've been a risky decision on his part, because his excessive drinking led to Mayall periodically firing him, replacing him at one point with future Cream member Jack Bruce. But Mayall clearly rated McVie's talent and inevitably rehired him. In the liner notes to the third Bluebreakers album *A Hard Road* (released in 1967 shortly before Fleetwood joined), Mayall wrote, 'Although John has been through good and bad times with us, I know from experience that a better blues bass guitarist would be difficult to find in this country.' Mayall also spoke highly of his group's lead guitarist Peter Green, writing that he 'would certainly cram Jimi Hendrix, Buddy Guy, Otis Rush, Eric Clapton and Peter Green on the same pedestal.' A further sign of the bandleader's regard for Green was a gift that – ironically – might've hastened the guitarist's departure from The Bluesbreakers. For Green's 20th birthday, Mayall gave him studio time to record on his own. With Fleetwood and McVie's backing, the guitarist recorded both sides of a single, and a trio of instrumentals. Green named one of them after his favorite rhythm section: 'Fleetwood Mac'.

Green's feelings notwithstanding, that rhythm section was split up – at least temporarily – when John Mayall fired Mick Fleetwood shortly after he joined the group, due to a non-musical affinity between the drummer and John McVie. As Fleetwood put it in his 1990 autobiography: 'I didn't have a drinking problem when I joined John Mayall, but I may have had one by the time I was fired. John Mayall probably realized that one drunken musician in the band was enough.'

Peter Green left The Bluesbreakers of his own volition in June 1967, intending to form a band where he could sidestep the guitar-hero image that Mayall chose to emphasize. Green wanted both Fleetwood and McVie to join the new group, which would take its name from the instrumental he named in their honour. But only the former joined initially, the latter preferring the relatively stable monetary situation playing for Mayall offered. While Green believed McVie would eventually join, they recruited bassist Bob Brunning in the short term and another guitarist. Jeremy Spencer was recommended to the group by Decca Records producer Mike Vernon, who'd formed Blue Horizon Records (to which the new band was signed) with his brother Richard.

Though the inclusion of a second guitarist stemmed in part from Green's desire not to be the centre of attention, the Vernons often billed the band as Peter Green's Fleetwood Mac. It was under this name that they played their first gig – a performance in August at the Seventh National Jazz and Blues Festival.

A precursor to the Reading Festival, the 1967 festival's lineup ranged from more-established groups like Cream and Pink Floyd (not to mention John Mayall and the Bluesbreakers) to a variety of newcomers. In addition to Fleetwood Mac, this included another band signed to Blue Horizon: Chicken Shack. The Birmingham-based group – who also played their first UK show at the Windsor Festival – included vocalist and keyboard player Christine Perfect. The 24-year-old art-school graduate also happened to be the daughter of a music teacher. While she didn't particularly care for classical piano in her younger years, she later developed a passion for blues. Perfect would also later develop personal and professional connections with Fleetwood Mac.

Before the year was out, and having become disenchanted with the musical direction John Mayall was pursuing, John McVie finally left The Bluesbreakers and joined Fleetwood Mac, as Peter Green had hoped.

Bob Brunning made way for McVie, and after playing with other bands, Brunning became a teacher and writer, with multiple books about his former band among his published work. Though Brunning played bass on the group's first single – a cover of Elmore James' 'I Believe My Time Ain't Long' – McVie played on the majority of their self-titled debut album. Released in February 1968, the album mixed Green and Spencer originals with songs by established blues artists such as Robert Johnson. It sold well in Britain, reaching number four on the album charts, and got good reviews. The non-album single 'Black Magic Woman' that followed the next month, was less successful, barely reaching the UK top 40, but had a second life in 1971 when San Francisco band Santana had a number-4 hit in the US with their recording of it.

1968 was eventful in general for Fleetwood Mac. After a brief tour of the United States, their second album *Mr. Wonderful* was released in August. Like their debut, it reached the UK top ten, but was noteworthy for including Christine Perfect's first appearance on a Fleetwood Mac album, contributing keyboards and vocals. She and John McVie – who'd been dating for some time – also got married that year. But Perfect remained with Chicken Shack for the time being, and Fleetwood Mac added another full-time member in the form of guitarist/singer Danny Kirwan.

In November 1968, Fleetwood Mac released their first and only number-1 single in the UK: the instrumental 'Albatross.' Peter Green's entrancing composition was an unmistakable signpost that the group had greater musical ambitions than simply emulating great American blues artists. Not that they were shying away from blues – after starting a US tour in December, (with a show opening for The Grateful Dead), they played a session with Buddy Guy and other American blues musicians at Chicago's Chess Studios in January. During this tour, they also recorded their next single 'Man Of The World', which was released in March 1969 and reached two on the British chart.

Danny Kirwan quickly found himself in the thick of things when Peter Green told him that half the songs on the next album would be Kirwan's to write and sing. Of the other seven songs on September's *Then Play On*, five were written by Green – including the infamous 'Rattlesnake Shake' – with relatively rare solo writing credits from both Fleetwood and McVie making up the balance. The album was another top-10 success in the UK, and made the lower half of the US album chart. The non-album single 'Oh Well' hit number two in Britain, and was the band's first charting single in America, where it reached 55.

Against that backdrop of musical success, Peter Green found himself struggling with both spiritual and earthly matters, and increasingly at odds with his bandmates personally and creatively. The turning point came when Green attended a party after a show in Munich, and took what others in the band believed was impure LSD. Though the break was now inevitable, Green still finished the tour. When they played the final show at the end of May, Green's final word with Fleetwood Mac had just entered the British charts. As menacing as 'Albatross' was graceful, 'The Green Manalishi (with the Two Prong Crown)' became Fleetwood Mac's last UK hit for several years.

Following the difficult situation with Green, the next several months brought happier times, at least temporarily. In June, Mick Fleetwood married his longtime girlfriend, Jenny Boyd. Boyd – who reputedly inspired Donovan's hit single 'Jennifer Juniper' – was the sister of Pattie Boyd Harrison, making Fleetwood George Harrison's brother-in-law. Meanwhile, after stepping back from music for a time and then recording a solo album that proved unsuccessful, Christine McVie accepted an invitation to join Fleetwood Mac. In August, she played her first show with the group, in New Orleans, Louisiana.

Because Christine was still under contract to the band's old label, she went uncredited on their next album. *Kiln House* – which was named after the country house the band and their families shared for several months – was less successful at home than their previous albums, but showed their audience gradually building in the United States.

The band's return to the US in February 1971 led to another lineup change when Jeremy Spencer disappeared shortly before a scheduled show in Los Angeles. After searching for several days, they found him at an L.A. warehouse, and learned that he'd joined a fringe religious sect called The Children of God. Whether this was willingly or the result of brainwashing, Spencer insisted to band manager Clifford Davis that he would not be rejoining Fleetwood Mac, and seemed similarly disinterested in his wife and children. Faced with the twin realizations that Spencer wasn't coming back and that canceling the remainder of the tour put them at risk of financial ruin, the band implored Peter Green to fly to America and help them get through the remaining dates. Green reluctantly agreed to help out his friends, and Fleetwood recalled the rest of the tour being successful, but also felt the sadness of knowing that these shows were 'the long goodbye.'

Losing a friend and longtime member under such unusual circumstances was hard on the band, but they did what they were best at: finding a new musical contributor to help evolve their sound. In April 1971, that individual was Bob Welch – a Californian living and working abroad, who also happened to be an excellent guitarist and strong songwriter. Even by the standard of later events, the period between Welch joining and his departure at the end of 1974 was particularly dynamic – the band recorded five albums and frequently toured, while two new members joined and three left: two of those under acrimonious circumstances.

Bob Welch was a stabilizing influence who contributed a great deal musically during his tenure – including two of the best songs the band ever recorded: 'Hypnotized' and 'Sentimental Lady' – and helped keep the band going during some troubled times. Though Welch didn't get along with Danny Kirwan, the actions which finally led to Kirwan being fired pointed to Welch not being the problem. Kirwan's replacements – Savoy Brown singer Dave Walker and Long John Baldry guitarist Bob Weston – ended up threatening the band's cohesion, and, in one case, much more than that.

Walker was pushed on the band by Clifford Davis, who felt Fleetwood Mac needed a traditional frontman. Unfortunately, Walker's onstage behavior (Mick Fleetwood described him as their first 'stereotypical lead singer') tended to draw focus away from the group as a whole. Conversely, his studio contributions were minimal – singing on only two songs for their early-1973 album *Penguin* (the first to incorporate the flightless bird imagery that's become so associated with the band). During sessions for the next album *Mystery to Me*, Walker's lack of engagement finally became too much, and he, too, was dismissed.

Mystery to Me embodied Fleetwood Mac as it was during Bob Welch's tenure. It was the sound of a band understanding that its future lay in the strength of their songwriting – much of it now coming from Christine McVie – and that they just needed to put the pieces together in the right combination. In the United States, fans seemed inclined to give the band time to accomplish this. Though by no means a blockbuster, *Mystery to Me* sold respectably, following the path of its immediate predecessors into the middle of the US album charts, eventually selling enough to be certified Gold. The situation was strikingly different in the UK, where none of their albums since *Kiln House* had charted at all. Even on the singles charts, Fleetwood Mac's only presence during this time was a 1973 'Albatross' re-release, which led to a televised moment that encapsulated how far the band had fallen off the cultural radar at home. The success of that reissue – which reached number two in the UK – led to 'Albatross' appearing on the BBC's *Top of the Pops*, during which the presenter erroneously commented that the group had broken up.

Fleetwood Mac had not broken up, but came very close in late 1973 as a result of marital indiscretions. The lack of personal space while living and working together, coupled with John's heavy drinking, amplified the existing troubles within the McVie's marriage, and led to Christine having an affair with band engineer Martin Birch. The couple decided to stay together, at least for a while longer. But Christine McVie wasn't the only band member involved in an extramarital affair.

In the case of Bob Weston, the problem wasn't the affair so much as who the affair was with. Mick Fleetwood later acknowledged that for many years he'd prioritized the needs of the band over his marriage and family. These elements collided on a US tour when he learned that Jenny was having an affair with Bob Weston. Though devastated by the revelation, the drummer resolved to preserve his marriage, and despite having to share the stage with his wife's lover, he pressed on with the tour until reaching an emotional breaking point during a show in Nebraska. After the band decided to part ways with Weston, road manager John Courage gave him a plane ticket back to England, and the news that his time with Fleetwood Mac was done.

The rest of the band had the more difficult task of explaining the situation and their need to postpone some of the upcoming concerts to Clifford Davis. Their soon-to-be-former manager reacted poorly in the moment, and even less well afterwards. Deciding he wasn't going to be 'brought down by the whims of irresponsible musicians,' Davis attempted to claim legal ownership of the name Fleetwood Mac, and hired a group of musicians to tour the United States under that name. Despite Fleetwood and company taking legal action, the structure of their contracts meant that the band's money flowed to Davis rather than to them. At the urging of Welch – who'd returned to Los Angeles after the incident with Weston – the other members relocated to the area so they could deal directly with their record company and hopefully start earning money again. Given the legal circumstances, before signing the band to a new record deal, Warner Bros. insisted that the band indemnify the label against any losses should the courts side with Davis.

Finally able to work again – at least in the US – Fleetwood Mac recorded *Heroes Are Hard to Find*, which in November 1974 became their first record to reach the top 40 there. While the legal case wouldn't be resolved for several years, the album's success seemed like a sign that Fleetwood Mac was back on track. However, after their tour ended in December, Welch told the band he was leaving. Unlike Kirwan or Weston's acrimonious departures, Welch's was on good terms, if a bit sudden. Feeling burnt-out after nearly a year as the band's *de facto* manager alongside Mick Fleetwood, Welch was also experiencing marital problems: in keeping with Fleetwood Mac tradition. His departure meant the band once again needed a guitarist. Fortunately, a November visit to the now-legendary Los Angeles studio Sound City had provided a lead on a replacement, and quite a bit more.

The subject of a 2013 documentary, the artists who have recorded at Sound City include the likes of Tom Petty and Nirvana. However, in its early days, the studio hosted a struggling duo who, in 1973, recorded one of the most consequential failed albums in pop music history. *Buckingham Nicks* – the debut record from 23-year-old singer-guitarist Lindsey Buckingham and 24-year-old singer Stevie Nicks – was the culmination of a multi-year collaboration that started in the San Francisco Bay area, before gravitating to Los Angeles, where the duo – who by this time were a couple – signed a record deal with Polydor. Their debut sold poorly everywhere except Birmingham, Alabama, but Buckingham and Nicks continued to push ahead, working with Sound City producer Keith Olsen. During Mick Fleetwood's visit to the studio, Olsen played him the Buckingham Nicks track 'Frozen Love,' to show off the studio's sound. The song stuck with the drummer, and after Welch's news, he contacted Olsen to get the name of the guitarist whose playing had impressed him so much. At the time, Fleetwood was only interested in Buckingham, but soon learned that the situation was more complex.

Buckingham recounted in a 2003 profile in *Uncut* magazine: 'He needed a guitar player. That was as far as his thinking went. I had to explain we came as a duo. Stupid me, eh?' The guitarist's loyalty to his partner was noteworthy, considering the low point in their collective fortunes. The duo had been struggling to make ends meet since moving to Los Angeles in 1971 after the dissolution of Fritz: the Bay Area band they were in together. Nicks took waitressing and cleaning jobs so Buckingham could focus on music: a dynamic that doubtless fed into some of the drama yet to come. After a few years of tough jobs, and the failure of their first album, she was at a crossroads. In the same *Uncut* piece, Nicks said, 'I was really tired of having no money and being a waitress. It's very possible that I would have gone back to school and Lindsey would have gone back to San Francisco.' Fortunately, an initial dinner meeting between the band and their prospective recruits, went well, and on New Year's Eve 1974, Buckingham and Nicks accepted the invitation to join Fleetwood Mac.

The latest incarnation of the nearly ten-year-old group started rehearsing early in the new year, and gelled very quickly. With Keith Olsen producing at Sound City, they soon recorded a new album, and before its release, they began one of the longest tours in their history. Having made just one album with the new lineup, their setlists mixed new songs with older Fleetwood Mac ones like 'Oh Well' and 'Hypnotized', alongside the Buckingham Nicks number 'Don't Let Me Down Again.' The new album *Fleetwood Mac* – which also drew the song 'Crystal' from the Buckingham Nicks record – was released during the tour. Today, the multiple top 20 singles and millions of copies sold, obscure the fact that the album wasn't an immediate hit. This was another way in which the new version of the band started out true to form for Fleetwood Mac. Prior to this album, Fleetwood Mac albums generally sold around 250,000 copies – enough to keep the band going but not enough to break through. It took over a year, but the band's persistence paid off when the album reached number 1 in America in September 1976. Nicks recalled: 'We just played everywhere and we sold that record. We kicked that album in the ass.'

Despite not touring in the UK at this point, it was the group's first album to chart there since *Kiln House* in 1970, and the renewed interest extended to the singles charts, with Christine McVie's 'Say You Love Me' becoming their first British top-40 hit since Peter Green's departure. McVie had been contributing songs to the band's albums for several years, but the new record provided public recognition of the ability one of her bandmates appreciated from the outset. In a 2004 interview, Christine said, 'When I joined Fleetwood Mac, it was Mick who encouraged me to write. I wrote a couple of songs on *Future Games* or *Bare Trees*.' Mick said, 'You should write more because you're pretty good.'

Adding Buckingham and Nicks after Bob Welch's departure meant the band now had a trio of strong songwriters, each with distinctive styles. McVie may have confined her subject matter to love and relationships, but few people were more accomplished at it. Meanwhile, Buckingham balanced pop sensibilities and an experimental streak, and Nicks crafted some of the most evocative songs of the era. Pieces like 'Rhiannon' worked in tandem with Nicks' stage presence and striking good looks, making her the group's breakout star. Though many suspected friction between the two female members, quite the opposite was true. McVie said in 2004: 'Stevie was this siren, this magic creature on stage. I was quite content to be behind the keyboards. I didn't want to compete with that at all. I was very happy with where I was.'

While the twists and turns in the band's history often invite suspicion of revisionist narratives, the keyboardist had said much the same thing In the 1970s. Interviewed for a 1976 piece in *Crawdaddy* magazine, she commented, 'Stevie's a showwoman and she loves it. I'm the keyboard player, which keeps me out of the limelight. I enjoy it because I'm not an extrovert.' In the same article, Nicks added, 'As for the dancing, it's nothing I haven't done my whole life. It's not a ploy to be sexy. I decided from the beginning that if I didn't have something visually interesting to do, I wouldn't stand out there.' Intentions aside, the end result was an abundance of male admirers – some quite famous – which added to existing tension in her relationship with Buckingham.

Because they started recording their next album before the current one topped the US charts, it was the last time commercial expectations for a new album by this incarnation would be so modest. It was also the first Fleetwood Mac album recorded with the same lineup as its predecessor since *Bare Trees* in 1972. However, that continuity didn't mean the group was particularly stable. In addition to the breakdown of Buckingham and Nicks' relationship, the problems that impacted Mick Fleetwood's marriage and that of the McVies, were – if anything – more pronounced than in 1973. Looking back many years later, Christine and John both recognized the role being in the band played in their divorce. Christine observed: 'When you're in the same band as somebody, you're seeing them 24 hours a day, and you start to see an awful lot of the bad side.' John McVie's comments were particularly revealing for someone who tended to be the least-vocal member of the band's most famous lineup:

Chris saw me at my worst one time too many. I drink too much, and when I've drunk too much, a personality comes out. It's not very pleasant to be around. And bless her heart, Chris said, 'I don't want to be around this person.' It was awful. You're told by someone you adore and love that they don't want you in their life anymore.

It would've been much simpler for all involved if *not* being in each other's lives had been a viable option, but the band members who'd stuck together through times when success seemed improbable, weren't likely to give up now that they'd achieved it. Their new bandmates shared a similar degree of commitment following their own struggles. Later events revealed their choices to be unhealthy in some respects, but in 1977, the quality of the music and the public reaction to it, justified their tenacity.

45 years of legendary status and record-breaking sales have somewhat obscured the extent to which genuine emotional turmoil fueled the *Rumours* album's irresistible portrait of relationships in crisis. For their part, Fleetwood Mac didn't shy away from it. Not only was the album title a direct reference to the public discussion of the band members' private lives, the first single, 'Go Your Own Way', put Lindsey Buckingham's feelings about Stevie Nicks on stark display as it headed for the US top 10. The subsequent singles 'Dreams,' 'Don't Stop' and 'You Make Loving Fun' were even more successful in the US (with 'Dreams' topping the chart), but were no less personal for Nicks and Christine McVie. The album's other songs also displayed the group's raw nerves: especially 'The Chain.' As the only song written collectively by the entire group in their time together, that song is sonic evidence of Mick Fleetwood's 1977 *New Musical Express* comment that 'Being in Fleetwood Mac is more like being in group therapy.'

The proximity by necessity continued when the band started touring the United States shortly after *Rumours* was released in February 1977. As sales exploded – making it one of the best-selling albums of all time – the individual band members attempted to move on personally, often in ways that made the comparisons of *Rumours* to watching a soap opera seem all the more apt. Christine McVie's affair with band lighting director Curry Grant continued even after Grant was fired, lasting until she began a three-year relationship with Dennis Wilson of The Beach Boys. Lindsey Buckingham indulged in various short-term flings before starting a multi-year relationship with Carol Ann Harris in 1978 – the same year John McVie married Julie Ann Reubens (who worked in Fleetwood Mac's office) with Mick Fleetwood serving as best man. Fleetwood and Jenny Boyd also remarried. However, the revelation of Mick's brief affair with Stevie Nicks ended this attempt at reconciliation, and Fleetwood soon started a relationship with Nicks' good friend Sara Recor, creating another rift in the band's orbit. Nicks was linked to many men (accurately and not) after her breakup with Buckingham: most prominently Eagles singer Don Henley.

Not long after *Rumours* received the Grammy award for Album of the Year in February 1978, Fleetwood Mac started work on their next album. The 1979 double album *Tusk* was many things – a case study in how the entertainment business judges success and failure by unusual measures, an elaborate penis joke, and the most ambitious record any iteration of Fleetwood Mac recorded, to name just a few. Above all, it was a concerted effort to avoid simply repeating the *Rumours* approach. Lindsey Buckingham – whose desire for musical experimentation, shaped the album's overall sound the most – has often joked that when Warner Bros. executives first heard *Tusk*, they 'saw their Christmas bonuses going out the window.' While that story is probably apocryphal, it speaks to the unusual place *Tusk* occupies in pop-music history. It was unrealistic to expect any album to be as popular as *Rumours*, which has sold over 40,000,000 copies since its release, and the idea that any double album that sells 4,000,000 copies is a failure seems wrongheaded. Nevertheless, despite being viewed more-favorably, in retrospect, *Tusk* wasn't what most record buyers wanted in October 1979. Public reaction was to set the stage for how the band worked together (and often didn't) over the next decade and beyond.

1980: When You Build Your House

Fleetwood Mac began the 1980s with the second single from *Tusk* – Stevie Nicks' ballad 'Sara' – ascending the charts around the world, reaching the top 10 in the United States. Inspired by the singer's relationships with Don Henley and Mick Fleetwood, and Fleetwood's relationship with Sara Recor, the breathtaking song was one of the few things about *Tusk* that listeners collectively agreed they enjoyed.

Many viewed the album as a whole as self-indulgent – a side effect of the more than 12 months and $1,000,000 spent making it. But it still contained undeniable moments of pop greatness. Presenting the work of multiple talented songwriters across an eclectic double album made comparisons to The Beatles' *White Album* inevitable and plentiful. Among the album's critics on its release, Greil Marcus offered one of the more distinctive reviews. In his 'Real Life Rock Top Ten' recap for 1979, in the magazine New West, Marcus described *Tusk* as 'radical in its refusal of the mainstream's limits.' He added a radical notion of his own, suggesting that 'Fleetwood Mac is subverting the music from the inside out, very much like one of John le Carré's moles who – planted in the heart of the establishment – does not begin his secret campaign of sabotage and betrayal until everyone has gotten used to him and takes him for granted.'

In hindsight, the album's initial perception as an unconventional or difficult record, was less about the music than the way audiences viewed its makers. Aside from a few outliers – mainly written by Lindsey Buckingham – the songs were no more unusual than a track like 'World Turning' from the 1975 *Fleetwood Mac* album. Considering that one of those oddities – the borderline-primal title track, featuring the University of Southern California's marching band – ranks among the band's biggest hits, it's hard to credit the idea that *Tusk* was an intrinsically unapproachable record. At the same time, the massive popularity of *Rumours* had shaped public expectations of what a Fleetwood Mac album should be, and *Tusk* undeniably confounded those expectations.

One of the most subtle aspects of the artistry of *Rumours* is how perfectly sequenced it is. 'Second Hand News,' 'Dreams' and 'Never Going Back Again' are strikingly different from each other, but each song plays off of those around it. The shift from one to the next – not to mention the remaining tracks on side one – never feels jarring. *Tusk* likewise opened with a diverse group of songs, but deliberately emphasized the contrast between tracks, veering from Christine McVie's graceful ballad 'Over & Over' into Buckingham's weirdly catchy 'The Ledge.' Side one also featured two legitimate hits – McVie's 'Think About Me' and the aforementioned 'Sara' – separated by Buckingham's 'Save Me A Place': a piece as gentle as 'The Ledge' was nervy.

This contrast, which continued over the album's next three sides, was another manifestation of Buckingham's embrace of the musical possibilities opened up by post-punk and new wave. In a 1981 profile for music magazine *BAM*, the guitarist observed that while he wasn't influenced by specific new wave artists, the general approach 'instilled a sense of courageousness in me and solidified a lot of the ideas I had about my music.' The shift of gears on his part was especially pronounced against the backdrop of Fleetwood Mac's dominant place in American pop music in the late-1970s, both within and outside of the band. In the period between *Rumours* and *Tusk*, every member of the group contributed to major hits by other artists. Buckingham and Christine McVie produced and played (along with Mick Fleetwood) on former member Bob Welch's 1977 remake of 'Sentimental Lady,' making the song the hit it always should've been. Buckingham and *Rumours* co-producer Richard Dashut produced Walter Egan's 'Magnet And Steel' with Nicks (who happened to be Egan's inspiration for the song) singing background vocals. Nicks also sang on Kenny Loggins' hit 'Whenever I Call You 'Friend,',' while Mick Fleetwood and John McVie played on Warren Zevon's 'Werewolves Of London.'

By accepting the challenge posed by the less-mainstream music that excited him at the time, Buckingham was placing his bet on future audiences. Based on the improved stature of *Tusk* within Fleetwood Mac's work over time, his bet paid off. However, before that reappraisal could take place, the band had a job to do. In February, they resumed the concert tour, which had started shortly after *Tusk* was released – an occasion marked by Los Angeles mayor Tom Bradley declaring 10 October 1979 as Fleetwood Mac Day; the band receiving a star on the Hollywood Walk of Fame.

While *Tusk* had failed to produce a Christmas windfall for Warner Bros. Records, no one can say the band themselves didn't do everything they could to boost the album's fortunes, playing over 100 shows across 11 countries. According reliable accounts, as well as those of band members, the tour was a case study in rock-star excess. Fleetwood – who also managed the band at the time – described this in both of his autobiographies. But his account in the first one – *Fleetwood: My Life and Adventures in Fleetwood Mac* (1991) – is more evocative:

> We ordered some of the priciest hotel suites in the world repainted in pastel shades for Stevie and Chris, and fabulous expense. The refreshment rider written into our contracts with the local promoters, provided an immense backstage buffet for an army of California gourmands, although many of us were too coked-up and glazed-over to actually eat anything. A king's ransom was spent on keeping the tour's cocaine supply adequate.

The substance abuse – which stood alongside music as a driving force for the *Tusk* tour – wasn't just limited to cocaine and marijuana. Christine McVie's well-documented fondness for champagne, continued on the road, while brandy was Fleetwood's drink of choice. By his own account, this didn't help his disposition when communicating with Sara – at one point arguing with her for hours on a transpacific phone call – and pointed to how chemical overindulgence was intertwined with another driving force of the tour: personal animosity. Not surprisingly, the most calamitous incident in this regard involved Lindsey Buckingham and Stevie Nicks. Describing the band's post-*Rumours* dynamic in a 2007 interview for *Performing Songwriter*, Nicks recounted: 'You went up on stage and tried to keep your problems off that stage, and then went back to separate dressing rooms and hotels and didn't go to the bar after the show, because you didn't even want to take a chance of having a run-in in front of people.' The limits of that approach were exposed at a 22 March 1980 show in Auckland, New Zealand, where the tension between her and Buckingham spilled over in front of the audience. It's generally accepted that during the show, Buckingham mocked Nicks and kicked her (behavior Mick Fleetwood attributed to the guitarist having 'hit the old scotch bottle a little too hard before the concert'), and Christine McVie slapped him and threw a drink in his face after the show. Beyond that, in another indelible example of Fleetwood Mac tradition, accounts of the event varied from one member to another, and over time. In a 1997 *Rolling Stone* feature, Nicks' description is very similar to Mick Fleetwood's from several years earlier:

> Lindsey and I had another huge thing that happened onstage in New Zealand. We had some kind of a fight, and he came over – might have

kicked me, did something to me, and we stopped the show. He went off, and we all ran at breakneck speed back to the dressing room to see who could kill him first. Christine got to him first, and then I got to him second; the bodyguards were trying to get in the middle of all of us.

Buckingham claims not to remember specifics, and quite possibly doesn't, but nor does he deny acting atrociously on the tour. When the incident came up in a 2003 band profile in *Mojo* magazine, he acknowledged, 'Oh, I wouldn't doubt that I mimicked Stevie onstage. And kicked her? That could have happened too.' Fuzzy recall aside, the guitarist disputes Nicks' more-recent description of events, which includes him throwing a guitar at her midway through the show, narrowly missing her but nevertheless angering not just McVie but everyone else with the band. In a 2007 *Mojo* article, Nicks said, 'Let's just say he was told by everybody – from tour manager to everybody involved – if you ever throw anything at her or kick her again, the crew will attack you and kill you.' Nicks punctuated her account by adding, 'It never happened again.'

For his part, Buckingham questioned whether the incident happened at all when asked about it for a 2013 *Daily Mail* article. While this piece included Christine McVie's comment, 'Oh, it happened, all right,' the evidence is unclear. That something awful happened at the Auckland show, has been known for a long time, yet it seems strange that such a vivid detail – especially one from a concert attended by tens-of-thousands of fans – would be such a relatively-late addition to the Fleetwood Mac legend. Likewise, where Nicks' 1997 and 2007 descriptions implied that McVie throwing the drink in Buckingham's face occurred at some point before the show's final song, other accounts suggest the altercation occurred post-concert. Whatever the specifics, Buckingham's actions were reprehensible, and he seems well aware that he was lucky not to follow in Danny Kirwan and Dave Walker's footsteps out of the band.

One thing that might help pin down what happened, or at least when it did, is surprising in its absence. There's no shortage of recordings from the *Tusk* tour in circulation, but none from the Auckland show. In any case, recording shows on the tour wasn't just the province of bootleggers, as the band itself had numerous concerts recorded in their entirety. After the tour finished in September with a show at the Hollywood Bowl, and relationships between band members were in a state where attempting to work on another album would've been counterproductive, Fleetwood Mac prepared to release their first official live album.

The band started recording concerts regularly on the *Rumours* tour, after Mick Fleetwood first suggested releasing a live album, and they continued the practice on the subsequent tour. While others in the band disliked the idea, Fleetwood kept pushing forward. In his role as manager, he doubtless appreciated the financial upside of a new release that required minimal production work. However, he also spoke of wanting a document of their prowess as a live band, telling a writer for Circus magazine: 'It seemed to me that after a year on the road, there was no better time to release one.' Buckingham was apparently the most opposed. But with his clout within the band diminished after the disappointing reception of *Tusk*, it's not surprising his objections were overruled. In a 1981 *Bam* interview, he told journalist Blair Jackson: 'I initially had some reservations about doing it, but now I'm glad we did. On this tour, we really came together as a band in ways that we hadn't before, and I feel that the versions of most of the songs we were playing were as good as any we'd done.'

Though *Live* served as a *de facto* greatest-hits collection, critical and commercial reception was mixed. Live albums – especially doubles – have rarely been critical favorites, and presumably many fans felt they had all the Fleetwood Mac music they needed by virtue of owning *Rumours* and *Fleetwood Mac*. Nevertheless, there were some reviewers who genuinely appreciated the collection's merits – such as Robert A. Hull, who reviewed it for *The Washington Post*: 'Even though each song was recorded at a different location, they flow into each other with such smooth continuity that the two-record set seems like a single inspired concert. 'Sara' – all seven minutes worth – is an absolute joy. Never has this band sounded more like Buddy Holly's Crickets backing up Jackie DeShannon.'

Live (1980)

Personnel:
Lindsey Buckingham: guitar, vocals
Mick Fleetwood: drums
Christine McVie: keyboards, vocals
John McVie: bass
Stevie Nicks: vocals
Additional personnel:
Ray Lindsey: guitar
Tony Todaro: percussion
Jeffery Sova: keyboards

Producers: Richard Dashut, Ken Caillat, Fleetwood Mac
Live recording/engineering: Ken Caillat, Biff Dawes, Trip Khaluf, Richard Dashut
Mixdown engineers: Ken Caillat, Richard Dashut
Release date: 8 December 1980
Chart places: US: 14, UK: 31
Running time: 83:00 (Original release)
Side One: 1. 'Monday Morning' (Buckingham), 2. 'Say You Love Me' (McVie), 3. 'Dreams' (Nicks), 4. 'Oh, Well' (Peter Green), 5. 'Over & Over' (McVie)
Side Two: 1. 'Sara' (Nicks), 2. 'Not That Funny' (Buckingham), 3. 'Never Going Back Again' (Buckingham), 4. 'Landslide' (Nicks)
Side Three: 1. 'Fireflies' (Nicks), 2. 'Over My Head' (McVie), 3. 'Rhiannon' (Nicks), 4. 'Don't Let Me Down Again' (Buckingham), 5. 'One More Night' (McVie)
Side Four: 1. 'Go Your Own Way' (Buckingham), 2. 'Don't Stop' (McVie), 3. 'I'm So Afraid' (Buckingham), 4. 'The Farmer's Daughter' (Brian Wilson, Mike Love)
2021 Reissue Bonus Disc:
1. 'Second Hand News' (Buckingham), 2. 'The Chain' (Fleetwood Mac), 3. 'Think About Me' (McVie), 4. 'What Makes You Think You're The One' (Buckingham), 5. 'Gold Dust Woman' (Nicks), 6. 'Brown Eyes' (McVie), 7. 'The Green Manalishi (With The Two Prong Crown') (Green), 8. 'Angel' (Nicks), 9. 'Hold Me' (McVie), 10 'Tusk' (Buckingham), 11. 'You Make Loving Fun' (McVie), 12. 'Sisters Of The Moon' (Nicks), 13. 'Songbird' (McVie), 14. 'Blue Letter' (Michael Curtis, Richard Curtis), 15. 'Fireflies' (Nicks)

Even before the expanded 2021 reissue, containing more than a dozen additional songs, *Live* made its case that there was more to Fleetwood Mac than radio-friendly pop. The 1980 performance of 'I'm So Afraid' included here was as strong a guitar showcase as anything from Peter Green's tenure – a period the current incarnation paid tribute to here with an energetic version of 'Oh Well.' The band continued playing this UK hit on a fairly regular basis after Green left, with Buckingham taking the lead vocal as of the 1975 tour. Another song that predated Buckingham and Nicks' time in the band was 'Don't Let Me Down Again.' Featured on the album in a live recording from 1975, it's one of the few currently available releases of a song from the *Buckingham Nicks* album.

Further differentiating their release from their peers' live albums, was a trio of new performances recorded live at private shows at the Santa Monica Civic Center in early September. Nicks and Christine McVie each offered solid-if-not-outstanding examples of their craft with 'Fireflies' and 'One More Night' respectively. 'Fireflies' was the more-captivating of the two. While the song only reached 60 in the United States and didn't chart at all in the UK or most other countries, it was a catchy addition to the catalog of songs inspired by the band's ongoing interpersonal dramas.

> Almost a breakdown of our love affair
> The stiletto cuts quick like a whip through the air
> Long-distance winners
> Will we survive the flight?
> Not one of us runs from the firelight

'One More Night' was a more downbeat affair, but nevertheless displayed McVie's gift for a striking turn of phrase.

> If you want her, better get her now
> Or she'll be running away somehow
> Oh, it's not for me to say
> If she'll be happy some other way

Rather than contributing a new song of his own, Buckingham paid tribute to one of his musical heroes: Brian Wilson. Wilson (whose brother Dennis was dating Christine McVie at the time) visited the studio during the making of *Tusk*. The visit was especially emotional for him, and Fleetwood Mac recording the lesser-known Beach Boys song 'Farmer's Daughter', from their second album *Surfin' U.S.A.*, was an audible signifier of the deep connection Buckingham felt for his musical idol. In a 2010 *Rolling Stone* piece, Buckingham wrote: '(The Beach Boys) may have sold the California dream to a lot of people, but for me, it was Brian Wilson showing how far you might have to go in order to make your own musical dream come true ... I've loved 'The Farmer's Daughter.' It's obscure enough and contemporary enough that I thought it would be good for us to cover.' The love for the already iconic Wilson was also on display in the live album's earnest dedication:

TO BRIAN: Thank you for THE FARMER'S DAUGHTER, you're the greatest.

The most significant Fleetwood Mac event in late 1980 would've been largely invisible to those outside the band's immediate orbit. After the

1973 split with Clifford Davis, the band decided to manage themselves. Mick Fleetwood took on much of the work in tandem with Bob Welch at first, then completely after Welch left, receiving an additional percentage of the profits via Seedy Management – the entity created to handle the band's business affairs. This put Fleetwood in the spotlight when accountants and representatives for the other members wanted to know why the *Tusk* tour had been far less profitable than expected. The qualities that made Mick an ideal manager when times were tough – especially his instincts for smoothing-over band conflicts – proved to be less beneficial where money was concerned. With no one outside the band in a position to say no to extravagances such as repainting a hotel room's walls to match a band member's taste, the drummer agreed to a multitude of on-the-road luxuries to keep them happy, regardless of the cost.

While accountants may not have appreciated the connection between less-than-legal substances and unaccounted-for money, the rest of the band surely did – especially Stevie Nicks and her new manager Irving Azoff. One of the music industry's most successful and imposing figures, Azoff first came to Los Angeles in 1972 with his client singer-songwriter Dan Fogelberg. Looking back on the era in Ronald Brownstein's 2021 book *Rock Me On the Water*, Azoff likened the 1980 music scene to the gold rush, and articulated the view that 'If you're really good in this business, you only have to be right once.' Having proven himself undeniably right with The Eagles, Azoff had placed a bet on Stevie Nicks as an artist in her own right outside of Fleetwood Mac, and aggressively turned the financial situation to his new client's advantage.

In addition to firing John Courage after a decade as the band's road manager, Mick was removed as manager – a move that wounded him, despite the others' assurances that it wasn't personal. Recounting these events in his 1990 and 2014 autobiographies, the degree of hurt was more palpable in the former, while the latter was, not surprisingly, more philosophical:

I received no piece of the publishing on our songs, and yet I worked every day to further the band. So to me, that percentage seemed fair, and my bandmates had agreed all these years. But that changed, and I suppose it was bound to once we reached the level that we did. Since that day, we've been a band ruled by democratic committee – sometimes for better, sometimes for worse.

Though probably not recognized at the time, this chain of events ensured that the remainder of the decade would be more about the band members' individual work than what they did together. Nicks had already told Fleetwood earlier in the year about her plans to make a solo album, but the band's decision to take an extended break before touring again or working on another album, cleared the way for other members to pursue their own projects. In spite of his often single-minded devotion to the band, this included Fleetwood, who made plans to start work on a solo album before the end of the year. But before that, he needed to address tax problems with the United States government, which led to him moving to Monte Carlo, foreshadowing further financial issues that emerged as the 1980s progressed.

Left: Fleetwood Mac's 1980 live album proved that their music wasn't just a studio creation. (*Warner Bros.*)

Right: *Mirage* offered fans a more straightforward, pop-oriented approach, in contrast to the sonic experiments of *Tusk*. (*Warner Bros.*)

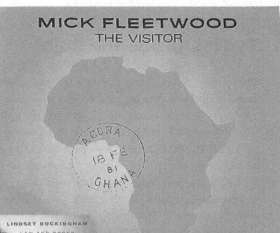

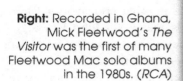

Right: Recorded in Ghana, Mick Fleetwood's *The Visitor* was the first of many Fleetwood Mac solo albums in the 1980s. (*RCA*)

Left: Lindsey Buckingham balanced an experimental attitude and a throwback musical feel on his first solo album, 1981's *Law and Order*. (*Asylum/Mercury*)

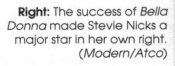

Right: The success of *Bella Donna* made Stevie Nicks a major star in her own right. (*Modern/Atco*)

1981: Outside the Rain

Once they collectively deciced to take a break from Fleetwood Mac, the band members quickly immersed themselves in other endeavours. Each released at least one solo album in the 1980s, except for John McVie, who limited his musical side-trips to some reunion gigs with John Mayall and The Bluesbreakers, and preferred to spend his downtime sailing, or at his home in Hawaii. Several of these records featured contributions from Fleetwood Mac members, and three were released in 1981 alone.

Considering how much effort Mick Fleetwood devoted to keeping the band together as relationships within it broke down over the previous decade, it's ironic that the first post-*Rumours* solo album was his. Because he was neither a singer nor songwriter (at least not on a regular basis), it's unsurprising that this record *The Visitor* was one of the bigger departures from the band's sound. Needing to decompress after the Bob Weston blow-up several years earlier, and after talking with Ghana-born ethnomusicologist and UCLA professor J. H. Kwabena Nketia, Mick flew to Zambia in December 1980. Becoming fascinated with African drumming, he wanted to record local musicians in their own communities. An arduous trip into the countryside to meet with Craig Woodson – an American scholar studying African rhythms in Ghana – revealed the need for Mick to rethink his plan. A combination of poor road conditions and a lack of reliable transportation (side effects of recent political and economic instability in the former British colony) made Fleetwood's initial idea unworkable. Instead – at Woodson's suggestion – Mick and longtime Fleetwood Mac lawyer Mickey Shapiro approached local studio owner Faisal Helwani about having musicians come to the country's capitol city Accra to record. A founding member of the Musicians Union of Ghana, Helwani (who died in 2008) was a key figure in Ghana's music scene, and something of a rogue in his approach to business. Fleetwood recalled that the price tag of Helwani's initial proposal nearly sank the project before it started, but they eventually made a deal to record with local artists on the soundstage at the Film Institute of Ghana. Though Mick had been an integral part of selling millions of records for Warner Bros., the label declined to fund the project's projected $500,000 cost. Fortunately, the aspect of filming the performances, appealed to RCA, who were eager to develop programming for the nascent home-video market.

In January 1981, Fleetwood returned to Accra, accompanied by musicians George Hawkins and Todd Sharp, producer Richard Dashut, a small crew, and a multitude of equipment, including a pair of 16-track tape-machines (in case the first one broke down). Seven weeks of recording culminated in an outdoor concert alongside the local musicians. He then flew to London, where he overdubbed additional musicians before returning to Los Angeles to complete overdubs and mix.

The Visitor wasn't the decade's first album to include western musicians collaborating with African artists, and certainly wasn't the best-selling. Its reception prefigured Police drummer Stewart Copeland's similarly-niche 1985 album *The Rhythmatist* more so than Paul Simon's *Graceland*, which became massively popular but also controversial following its 1986 release. In a 1998 Fleetwood Mac biography by original bassist Bob Brunning, Mick was quoted as saying, 'I went there hoping to leave something behind – not just to rip off the African musicians. I wanted to put something into the country, not just *take out*.' In spite of those good intentions, when *The Visitor* was released in June 1981, it stalled outside the US Top 40 and didn't chart in the UK.

The Visitor (Mick Fleetwood) (1981)

Personnel:
Mick Fleetwood: drums, percussion, water gong
George Hawkins: vocals, bass, piano, organ, guitar
Todd Sharp: lead and rhythm guitar
Lord Tiki: hand drums
Ebaali Gbiko: hand drums, backing vocals
Accra Romam Catholic Choir: backing vocals
Superbrains: percussion
Adjo Group, The Ghana Folkloric Group: vocals, percussion
Additional personnel:
Peter Green: lead guitar and vocals ('Rattlensake Shake'), theme guitar ('Super Brains')
George Harrison: guitars, backing vocals ('Walk A Thin Line')
Ian Bairnson: guitars ('Not Fade Away', 'Cassiopeia Surrender')
Richard Dashut: additional percussion ('Rattlesnake Shake')
Sara Fleetwood: backing vocals ('Walk A Thin Line')
Mike Moran: synthesizer ('The Visitor')
Andrew Powell: string arrangement ('Rattlesnake Shake', 'You Weren't In Love')
Producers: Mick Fleetwood, Richard Dashut
Executive producer: Mickey Shapiro
Engineers: Bill Youdelman, Randy Ezratty, Richard Dashut

Release date: June 1981
Chart places: US: 43, UK: N/A
Running time: 38:34
Side One: 1. 'Rattlesnake Shake' (Peter Green), 2. 'You Weren't In Love'
(Billy Field), 3. 'O' Niamali' (Nii Amartey), 4. 'Super Brains' (A. B. Crentsil),
5. 'Don't Be Sorry, Just Be Happy' (Todd Sharp)
Side Two: 1. 'Walk A Thin Line' (Buckingham), 2. 'Not Fade Away' (Charles
Hardin, Norman Petty), 3. 'Cassiopeia Surrender' (George Hawkins), 4. 'The
Visitor' (C. K. Ganjo), 5. 'Amelie (Come On Show Me Your Heart)' (Nii Amartey)

Despite the alternate musical approach, Fleetwood Mac still exerted
an influence on *The Visitor*, which opened with a new rendition of
'Rattlesnake Shake': Peter Green's ode to Onanism from *Then Play On*.
Asked to list favorites from his body of work for a 1995 *Mojo* feature,
Mick Fleetwood singled out this recording, which seems fitting since
Green wrote the song about the drummer's 'ample habits as a young
masturbatory male.' Discussing Green's contribution to the track,
Fleetwood recalled, 'I even got Peter to add a little bit of guitar at the very
end. It's that same old magic one-note reverb sound just put in the right
place, and of course, he sang it.'

Vocals for many other songs on the album came from bass player
George Hawkins, including the yearning ballad 'You Weren't In Love.' The
track was released as a single, but didn't make much of an impression in
terms of airplay or sales. This was in stark contrast to the version released
by the song's composer – Australian singer-songwriter Billy Field – which
reached number 1 in Australia and charted in New Zealand and the UK.

The infectious 'Oh Niamali' is one of two of the album's songs written
by Gilbert 'Nii' Amartey of Ghanian band Edikanfo, who were part of
the lineup for the concert Fleetwood staged in Accra during the album's
recording. Edikanfo was managed by Faisal Helwani, who invited Brian
Eno to produce an album for them. Eno – who'd recently produced Talking
Heads' African-influenced album *Remain in Light* – accepted the invitation,
and the Edikanfo album *The Pace Setters* was released internationally in
1981. Unfortunately, Edikanfo split up after political upheaval in Ghana
derailed their plans for a world tour, and after regrouping in recent years,
their renewed intentions to tour collided with the COVID-19 pandemic.

'Super Brains' shares the name of a Ghanaian artist performing on the
album (and this track), and was composed by A. B. Crentsil. Born in 1943
when Ghana was still the British colony known as the Gold Coast, Crentsil

was a prolific and enduring purveyor of highlife music – a long-standing Ghanian style melding traditional African music with jazz and other international influences. 'Super Brains' grooves along nicely, with Peter Green's guitar interjections giving the recording a unique atmosphere.

Side one finishes with another piece of local origin, albeit a track of a different kind. In his 1991 autobiography, Mick Fleetwood noted that guitarist Todd Sharp (who previously played with Bob Welch) wrote 'Don't Be Sorry, Just Be Happy' based on slogans he saw on the back of local buses. The arrangement is distinguished by the subtle percussion touches throughout.

What was a more-recent Fleetwood Mac song opens side two. This rendition of Buckingham's 'Walk A Thin Line' – featuring Mick Fleetwood's former brother-in-law George Harrison on guitar – managed the paradoxical trick of being both faster *and* more easygoing than the version on *Tusk*. In the liner notes for a reissue of Fleetwood Mac's 1982 album *Mirage*, Fleetwood described playing this version for Buckingham. 'I remember sitting Lindsey down and playing him that song, and that he was really moved hearing our crazy band from Africa doing one of his tracks'.

The rock-and-roll standard 'Not Fade Away' is among the most recorded and performed songs of the rock era. Originally recorded by Buddy Holly – who co-wrote it under the name Charles Hardin – the song was also a hit for The Rolling Stones. Fleetwood's recording calls to mind the Stones' beat-heavy version, which in 1963 became their first top-10 UK single. The song's presence on the album is fitting, since the Bo Diddley beat that drives it has roots in traditional African music.

The driving rhythm of 'Cassiopeia Surrender' neatly counterpoints George Hawkins' lyric. The song also makes a valuable point about *The Visitor*. While Hawkins and Todd Sharp weren't songwriters or players on the level of Buckingham or Christine McVie, they were talented and worthy collaborators for Mick Fleetwood. Both contributed to subsequent Fleetwood Mac solo projects as performers and writers.

All this waiting brings her down
So she makes some reservations at a cozy place in town
And she goes out on a bender
Cassiopeia surrender

After this trio of rock-oriented songs, the focus returns to African styles for the last two songs. The title track by C. K. Ganjo featured the Ghana

35

Folkloric Group, lauded by Fleetwood as 'some of the best harmony singers I ever heard.' It's followed by another Nii Amartey song: the enticing 'Amelie (Come On Show Me Your Heart).' Like the album's other Amartey song, 'O' Niamali,' it features local vocal ensemble Adjo Group.

The Visitor almost certainly didn't recoup RCA's investment, but Mick Fleetwood remained fond of the record, and spoke appreciatively of how the process of making it under trying circumstances was a counterweight to his admittedly decadent rock-star life. His considerable pride in the project came through in the liner notes:

I could not have wished to have been with better people in every way before, during and after the making of this album. Thank you all for making a not-easy endeavor a reality. Being a visitor to Ghana will be a heartfelt memory with me for the rest of my life.

Bella Donna – Stevie Nicks (1981)

Personnel:
Side One:
1. 'Bella Donna' (Stevie Nicks)
Stevie Nicks: lead vocals, Sharon Celani, Lori Perry: backing vocals, Russ Kunkel: drums, Davey Johnstone: acoustic guitar, Bob Glaub: bass, Bill Elliott: piano, Bobbye Hall: percussion, Benmont Tench: organ, David Adelstein: synthesizer
2. 'Kind Of Woman' (Stevie Nicks; musical bridge by Benmont Tench)
Stevie Nicks: lead vocals, Sharon Celani, Lori Perry: backing vocals, Russ Kunkel: drums, Davey Johnstone: acoustic guitar, Roy Bittan: piano, Benmont Tench: organ, Bob Glaub: bass, Bobbye Hall: percussion, Waddy Wachtel: guitar
3. 'Stop Draggin' My Heart Around' (Tom Petty, Michael Campbell)
Stevie Nicks: lead vocals, Sharon Celani, Lori Perry: backing vocals, Tom Petty: guitar, vocals, Benmont Tench: organ, Michael Campbell: guitar, Duck Dunn: bass, Stan Lynch: drums, Phil Jones: percussion
4. 'Think About It' (Stevie Nicks; musical bridge by Roy Bittan)
Stevie Nicks: lead vocals, Sharon Celani, Lori Perry: backing vocals, Russ Kunkel: drums, Waddy Wachtel: guitar, Davey Johnstone: acoustic guitar, Bob Glaub: bass, Bobbye Hall: percussion, Benmont Tench: organ, Billy Payne: piano
5. 'After the Glitter Fades' (Stevie Nicks)
Stevie Nicks: lead vocals, Sharon Celani, Lori Perry: backing vocals, Russ Kunkel: drums, Waddy Wachtel: guitar, Davey Johnstone: acoustic guitar, Bob Glaub: bass, Bobbye Hall: percussion, Roy Bittan: piano, Benmont Tench: organ, Dan Dugmore: pedal steel guitar

Side Two:
1. 'Edge of Seventeen' (Stevie Nicks)
Stevie Nicks: lead vocals, Sharon Celani, Lori Perry: backing vocals, Russ
Kunkel: drums
Bob Glaub: bass, Waddy Wachtel: guitar, Bobbye Hall: percussion, Roy Bittan:
piano, Benmont Tench: organ
2. 'How Still My Love' (Stevie Nicks)
Stevie Nicks: lead vocals, Sharon Celani, Lori Perry: backing vocals, Russ Kunkel:
drums, Waddy Wachtel: guitar, Davey Johnstone: acoustic guitar, Bob Glaub:
bass, Bobbye Hall: percussion, Roy Bittan: piano, Benmont Tench: organ
3. 'Leather And Lace' (Stevie Nicks)
Stevie Nicks: lead vocals, Sharon Celani, Lori Perry: backing vocals, Don
Henley: vocals, Waddy Wachtel: guitar, Roy Bittan: piano, Russ Kunkel: drums
4. 'Outside The Rain' (Stevie Nicks)
Stevie Nicks: lead vocals, Sharon Celani, Lori Perry: backing vocals, Tom
Petty: guitar, Michael Campbell: guitar, Benmont Tench: organ, Tom
Moncrieff: bass, Stan Lynch: drums, Phil Jones: percussion
5. 'The Highwayman' (Stevie Nicks)
Stevie Nicks: lead vocals, Sharon Celani, Lori Perry: backing vocals, Don Henley:
drums, background vocals, Don Felder: guitar, Michael Campbell: guitar,
Benmont Tench: organ, Richard Bowden: bass, Davey Johnstone: acoustic guitar
2016 Deluxe Edition – Disc Two: Bonus tracks
1. 'Edge Of Seventeen' (Early take) (Nicks), 2. 'Think About It' (Alternate
version) (Nicks, Bittan), 3. 'How Still My Love' (Alternate version) (Nicks),
4. 'Leather And Lace' (Alternate version) (Nicks), 5. 'Bella Donna' (Demo)
(Nicks), 6. 'Gold And Braid' (Unreleased version) (Nicks, Tom Moncrieff),
7. 'Sleeping Angel' (Alternate Version) (Nicks) 8. 'If You Were My Love'
(Unreleased version) (Nicks), 9. 'The Dealer' (Unreleased version) (Nicks),
10. 'Blue Lamp' (from Heavy Metal soundtrack) (Nicks), 11. 'Sleeping Angel'
(from Fast Times At Ridgemont High soundtrack) (Nicks)
2016 Deluxe Edition – Disc Three: Live At Fox Wiltshire Theatre, 13 December 1981
1. 'Gold Dust Woman' (Nicks), 2. 'Gold And Braid' (Nicks, Moncrieff), 3. 'I
Need To Know' (Tom Petty), 4. 'Outside The Rain' (Nicks), 5. 'Dreams' (Nicks),
6. 'Angel' (Nicks), 7. 'After The Glitter Fades' (Nicks), 8. 'Leather And Lace'
(Nicks), 9. 'Stop Draggin' My Heart Around' (Petty, Campbell), 10. 'Bella
Donna' (Nicks), 11. 'Sara' (Nicks), 12. 'How Still My Love' (Nicks), 13. 'Edge of
Seventeen' (Nicks), 14. 'Rhiannon' (Nicks)
Personnel: Stevie Nicks: lead vocals, Sharon Celani, Lori Perry: backing vocals,
Roy Bittan: piano

Bob Glaub: bass, Bobbye Hall: percussion, Russ Kunkel: drums, Benmont
Tench: keyboards, synthesizer, Waddy Wachtel: guitar
Original album producers: Jimmy Iovine; Tom Petty ('Stop Draggin' My Heart
Around' and 'Outside The Rain')
Engineer: Shelly Yakus
Musical director: Benmont Tench
Release date: 27 July 1981
Chart places: US: 1, UK: 11
Running Time: 41:55 (Original release)

Though Christine McVie wrote more of the band's hits, and Buckingham
played a larger role in shaping its overall sound, Stevie Nicks was clearly
the breakout star of Fleetwood Mac. Her first solo album *Bella Donna* and
a quartet of top-40 US singles, cemented this from a public standpoint,
but the album's significance to her was more personal. Beyond needing
space from Fleetwood Mac after a long, fractious tour, Nicks needed an
outlet for her songs. She told journalist Sylvie Simmons in a 1981 *Kerrang!*
magazine interview: '(With Fleetwood Mac) there's only one album every
two or three years, and as a writer, two or three songs every two or three
years is not much. I write all the time – sometimes three or four a month –
so I have such an incredible backlog of material that there's no reason for
me to ever have to write another song.'

One upside of this wealth of unrecorded songs accumulated over a
decade, was that it made *Bella Donna* a portrait of the singer's life. Not
that this was her intention, as she told Blair Jackson in a 1981 *BAM*
magazine interview: 'I didn't pick out the songs on *Bella Donna* because
I wanted to document my life. I picked them because I liked them. It just
sort of worked out that way.'

While some of the individual songs were older, the origins of
Bella Donna extended back to 1976 when Nicks, on the advice of
her parents, hired Irving Azoff as her manager, and formed her own
record label. She established Modern Records with help from former
Led Zeppelin publicist Danny Goldberg (later Nirvana's manager) and
former Bearsville Records President Paul Fishkin, securing distribution
through Atlantic Records in 1980. Aside from the songs themselves,
the album was defined by the answer to a question posed by Atlantic
President Doug Morris, as Nicks recounted in a conversation for a
2016 re-release: 'Doug said to me, 'Who do you want to produce
your record?' I said, 'I want whoever produces Tom Petty and the

Heartbreakers. If I can't be *in* the Heartbreakers, at least I can get Tom's producer so I can make the girl version of what I love about Tom Petty.' And Doug said, 'Well, that's Jimmy Iovine. I'll set you up.'

Jimmy Iovine engineered records by John Lennon and Bruce Springsteen in the mid-1970s before producing Tom Petty and the Heartbreakers' 1979 breakthrough *Damn the Torpedoes*. An initial dinner meeting between Nicks and Iovine was the prelude to a personal relationship and a professional one. Aside from the risks of being romantically involved with those you work with, Iovine was well aware of the musical challenge that working with Nicks posed: 'The biggest challenge of *Bella Donna* for me was having someone coming out of the gigantic rock band that have big hits and total credibility, and to have to create a sound behind the voice of one of the singers.' Gifted with a strong collection of songs, Iovine understood the importance of assembling the right group of musicians to support that singer. To this end, he recruited players comfortable in a band environment, such as Roy Bittan, Waddy Wachtel and various members of the Heartbreakers. Iovine explained in the 2016: 'I used musicians from bands, 'cause studio guys, their thing can fit on anything, and they become sometimes very neutral-sounding ... Everybody I used had to have a real distinct sound.'

Since these musicians were also busy, producer and artist had to work around their other commitments, requiring a mix of patience and preparation. While Iovine finished work on The Heartbreakers' album *Hard Promises* – which had Nicks singing on two tracks – Nicks spent two months working through the songs with background vocalists Sharon Celani and Lori Perry and Heartbreakers keyboardist Benmont Tench. Nicks told Chris Neal from *Performing Songwriter*: 'We played and sang all the songs on *Bella Donna* over and over until we had them down perfect. It was so much fun. We were like Joni Mitchell and Crosby, Stills & Nash, living in this great house and making music in Laurel Canyon.'

That balance between work ethic and freewheeling enthusiasm ensured that the recording of the album was efficient but not sterile. Nicks also enjoyed the freedom to arrange songs to her taste without getting bogged down in creative negotiations with Lindsey Buckingham. Nicks explained to Blair Jackson: 'On this album, I didn't have to fight to do my songs the way I wanted to. The other players just did them the way I wrote them, and they came out great. We didn't do a ton of overdubs. We didn't put on 50,000 guitars, because we didn't have Waddy around long enough to do 50,000 guitar overdubs. We were lucky to get him to do *one* guitar part.'

Reviews were mixed, but the record was an instant hit with audiences. Preceded by the single 'Stop Draggin' My Heart Around,' – a duet with Tom Petty – the album quickly topped the US charts, selling over 1,000,000 copies in less than three months. Nicks looked back on the album as a reflection of her love story with Jimmy Iovine, and observers such as Doug Morris believe that relationship added 'a lot of passion to the record.' Whatever listeners responded to, the element that distinguishes *Bella Donna* from many of Nicks' later solo albums, is how cohesively it portrays her as a person and performer. At its core, is the high level of songwriting (with only one song not written by Nicks), which felt every bit as personal as *Rumours*, putting her even closer to singer-songwriter territory than she got with Fleetwood Mac.

The piano-driven title track sets the tone for the album, with a balance of immediacy and reflection. Nicks' decision to call the record *Bella Donna* came out of a trip to Chile she took shortly after the completion of *Tusk*, with her then-boyfriend, engineer Hernan Rojas. Meeting Rojas' extended family there, the singer developed a particular bond with Rojas' mother Maria Teresa, which he described in *Get Tusked*: the 2019 book he co-wrote with frequent Fleetwood Mac collaborator Ken Caillat about the making of *Tusk*: 'Stevie connected with my other Maria Teresa deeply, as they both shared a similar character: sensitive, romantic and given to enjoy melancholic moments. They hung out and talked about memories and wisdom until dawn, resulting in Stevie writing her letters that she would leave under her door.'

One of those letters included the plea, 'Never let anyone take love and goodness away from you – never stop, never change.' Nicks echoes that sentiment in the song 'Bella Donna' when she sings, 'Don't change/Baby please don't change.' Nicks gave Maria Teresa the nickname Belladonna. It was initially a reference to an ingredient in a remedy the older woman gave the singer, which could be poisonous in too large a quantity. Nicks became fond of the double meaning of 'beautiful woman' and a deadly poison, seeing that 'double-edged sword' as analogous to her ambiguous position between the known quantity of Fleetwood Mac and a possible career as a solo artist.

'Bella Donna' is followed by one of the record's older compositions. The musical underpinning of 'Kind Of Woman', is the piano/guitar interplay of Benmont Tench and Waddy Wachtel, while Nicks' lyric and vocal are a testament to one of pop music's most enduring subjects: desire. More specifically, it reflected desire's dark side: jealousy. On the American radio program *Rockline*, she talked about writing the song after Lindsey Buckingham accepted an offer to tour with The Everly Brothers – Nicks imagining the temptations being on the road might present.

> I promised myself a long time ago
> It would be difficult to let you go
> If not at least within the touch of my fingers
> It was close to being in heaven

While Nicks prized *Bella Donna* as an outlet for her songs, she was willing to make an exception by including Tom Petty. Nicks had pleaded with Petty to write a song for her, and according to some, had wanted him to produce the album prior to being introduced to Jimmy Iovine. The song Petty wrote for her was 'Insider' – a ballad that prompted the producer to declare, 'That's the best fucking song you ever wrote.' Though they recorded 'Insider' together, it was ultimately released on Petty's album *Hard Promises* – the title of which comes from 'Insider'. Around the time of the *Hard Promises* release, Petty told *Rolling Stone* that Nicks insisted he keep the song. But in a later interview for *American Songwriter* magazine, he recalled being the one to insist on keeping 'Insider'.

Whichever account is accurate, both culminate in Nicks recording a different song with Tom Petty and the Heartbreakers: 'Stop Draggin' My Heart Around'. Written by Petty and Heartbreakers guitarist Mike Campbell, the song addressed Jimmy Iovine's concern that as good as the songs that Stevie planned to record were, they didn't include the hit that would make the album essential listening. Here again, different stories have been told about how this particular song came to be the one, but the end result indisputably validated the producer's instinct. Alternating between kiss-off and come-hither, the end result reached number three on the US singles chart, and remains the biggest hit of both Nicks and Petty's careers. On a commentary track for the song's music video, Nicks mused that, '(Petty) could've changed history if he'd just asked me to be in the Heartbreakers then, and we could've avoided all the rest of the problems with Fleetwood Mac.'

> It's hard to think about what you you've wanted
> It's hard to think about what you've lost
> This doesn't have to be the big 'get even'
> This doesn't have to be anything at all

The two singers' audible chemistry, sparked speculation about the nature of their relationship. Nicks dispatched the notion of any romantic element in 1981 when asked about the prospect of further collaboration: 'Tom and I aren't in love with each other, or haven't been in love and out of love. We're really just good friends, so we probably could write together.' Though they didn't end up writing together, the pair continued to record and perform periodically. In 1981, this included several concert appearances with Petty and the band, singing 'Stop Draggin' My Heart Around', 'Insider' and the 1960s classic 'Needles And Pins'.

Fleetwood Mac may have been a known quantity in Nicks' musical life, but the album's next song reflected that this was not synonymous with being a stable one. Lyrics such as 'Heartbreak of the moment is not endless/ Your fortune is your life's love' are consistent with the singer's other reflections on life and love. In this instance, the song wasn't specifically about her own experiences, but rather Christine McVie's in the mid-1970s, as her relationship with John McVie was breaking down offstage, and their onstage one wasn't much healthier. Nicks wrote in 2016: 'There was a point where she'd really had it with Fleetwood Mac. So I'm saying, 'Think about it, before you go, even when you feel like your heart is breaking'.'

The source of inspiration for side one's closing track, 'After The Glitter Fades', was a return to Nick's own life. An affecting song about the downside of fame, and the oldest one on the album, it would've been remarkable had Nicks written it about her life in Fleetwood Mac, but was all the more so because its composition predated her and Buckingham joining the band. In an interview with New York radio station WLIR, she mused that the piece was, 'A strange premonition to have in 1972 because it was two years before Fleetwood Mac. And that was when the *Buckingham Nicks* album had been dropped. So we were going nowhere. Fast.' While she might not have had the facts at hand yet, she innately understood the truth of the matter.

> Even though the living
> Is sometimes laced with lies
> It's alright,
> The feeling remains
> Even after the glitter fades

With the song's country feel, it's not surprising that Nicks told an interviewer for Philadelphia radio station WMMR that she'd wanted

Dolly Parton to record it: 'It got sent to her, and I don't think Dolly ever really got it. And I think, if she ever really got the song, she would've wanted to do it.'

If forced to pick one song that defined Stevie Nicks as an artist, it would be hard to surpass the opening track of *Bella Donna*'s second side: 'Edge Of Seventeen'. Though the first two singles from the album were bigger hits, 'Edge Of Seventeen' encapsulates her musical and lyrical approach better than anything else on the record.

I went today
Maybe I will go again tomorrow
And the music there, it was hauntingly familiar
And I see you doing what I try to do for me
With the words from a poet
And a voice from a choir
And a melody
Nothing else mattered

The song was sparked by the deaths of her uncle Jonathan and John Lennon. In a 1981 *Rolling Stone* feature, Nicks explained: 'The white-winged dove in the song is a spirit that's leaving a body, and I felt a great loss at how both Johns were taken.' At the same time, the song drew accidental inspiration from something that was very much alive: the marriage of Tom and Jane Petty. When Jane told Nicks about meeting Tom Petty at 'the age of 17', Nicks misheard it as 'the edge of seventeen'. The emotions at the song's core were highlighted by a piece of musical invention that made her rethink how to approach its recording. She wrote in the liner notes for the 2007 compilation *Crystal Visions*: 'It would've been one of my piano songs if Waddy Wachtel hadn't come into the studio and added the amazing guitar riff at the beginning of the song.' Collectively, those highly-specific inspirations struck a universal chord, and 'Edge of Seventeen' became Nicks' signature song and the perennial closing number for her solo concerts.

Album placement after 'Edge of Seventeen' highlights how 'How Still My Love' has the least substantial lyric of any song on *Bella Donna*. Aside from 'You go, your way' and the associations that phrase carries, most of the lines come across as marking time between Nicks' singing, 'In the still of the night/How still my love.' Fortunately, she sings those lines with more conviction than they warrant, and the band matches her intent.

Sung with Don Henley, 'Leather And Lace' is the polar opposite to the album's other high-profile duet. Heartfelt and gentle, 'Leather And Lace' was written in 1976 when country music icon Waylon Jennings asked Nicks to write a song he could record with his wife: singer Jessi Colter. Though their relationship faced some difficult times, Jennings and Colter remained together until Jennings died in 2002. One of those troubled periods led to Nicks reclaiming the song for *Bella Donna*. According to a 1982 piece in European magazine *Rock*, 'Waylon decided he was going to do it alone. But I said no, because I put a lot of time into the psychology of the song and felt it was a mistake to do it alone.' Henley singing on her recording was doubly appropriate. Not only did he serve as a sounding board (and taskmaster) while she was writing it, he also sang on a demo that Nicks described in a radio interview as, 'So similar to the record, that a lot of people don't even notice it if I put the demo on.'

Nicks referred to 'Leather And Lace' as a very disciplined song, because she knew she had to finish it for Jennings. That adjective applies to its content as well. The structure of the verses is deliberate, with these lines in the initial verse:

Still I carry this feeling
When you walked into my house
That you won't be walking out the door

…directly responded to in these that follow the chorus…

And you were right
When I walked into your house
I knew I'd never want to leave

As with Tom Petty and 'Stop Draggin' My Heart Around,' Nicks and Henley periodically reprised their duet onstage over the years.

Despite 'Outside The Rain' being recorded with Tom Petty and the Heartbreakers, Stevie Nicks also had another band in mind for it. She told Sylvie Simmons: 'It was the only link between Fleetwood Mac and me. It was the song they would've done if they were involved in the record. It was the 'Dreams' or the 'Sara'.' The energy of the recording is pure Heartbreakers, but it doesn't take a lot of pondering to envision the lyric being directed at Lindsey Buckingham.

So you're still lonely
You say that it's been forever
Maybe you never knew me
Maybe thought that I'd never change
But you know I'm changing
You're wrong

Like side one of *Bella Donna*, side two ends with a song Nicks had written years earlier. 'The Highwayman' took a more-overtly poetic approach than 'After The Glitter Fades,' but was no less personal. Nicks explained for a *Smash Hits* piece in 1982: 'It's about what a woman in rock-and-roll has to do to keep up with the men. It's their world. To be taken seriously, a woman has to walk softly and carry a big stick.' Hindsight (and a variety of biographies) points to the folly of romanticizing both Nicks' generation of rock stars and the outlaw legends of the past she equates them to. Nonetheless, her lyrics come across as thoroughly sincere in considering both sides of the relationship.

And she wonders is this real
Or does she just want to be queen
And he fights the way he feels
Is this the end of the dream?

While the prevalence of deluxe reissues – celebrating established artists instead of fostering new talent - isn't entirely healthy for the music industry, the best of them provide valuable insight into the making of enduring favorites. The 2016 reissue of *Bella Donna* offered added perspective on Nicks as a songwriter and performer. Along with alternative recordings of songs from the album, and some compositions she was to revisit for later records, it featured two strong tracks recorded for movies. 'Sleeping Angel' appeared on the soundtrack for *Fast Times at Ridgemont High*, and 'Blue Lamp' – the first song recorded during the sessions – was used in a segment of *Heavy Metal*; the soundtrack album's executive producer being Nicks' manager Irving Azoff.

The third disc of the set was recorded on 13 December 1981 at the final concert of Nicks' brief tour to promote *Bella Donna*. The show was recorded for HBO, but only nine of the 16 tracks were included in the broadcast and the following home-video *White Wing Dove – Stevie Nicks in Concert*. The CD release was still sightly abridged – omitting

'Blue Lamp' and 'Think About It' – but nevertheless proved that Nicks was capable of carrying a show on her own, even if commitments to Fleetwood Mac meant she had to put her solo work aside for a while.

In recent years, Nicks has presented a narrative of going right from the end of her tour into recording sessions with Fleetwood Mac in France. While it's likely that work with the band followed her solo shows in short order, most reliable accounts place the initial recording sessions for what became *Mirage* as being much earlier in 1981. While none of the other Fleetwood Mac members performed on *Bella Donna* or Mick Fleetwood's *The Visitor,* Christine McVie broke the mold by recruiting Lindsey Buckingham to play on her own solo project that year, albeit a different sort of venture than those of her bandmates. Rather than recording an album of her own, McVie produced one for English singer-songwriter Robbie Patton, who opened for Fleetwood Mac on the *Tusk* tour. That album *Distant Shores* sold poorly, but had one commercial bright spot in the single 'Don't Give It Up', which reached 26 in the US in August. In addition to Buckingham, the track featured former Fleetwood Mac guitarists Bob Weston and Bob Welch.

In November, Welch invited Patton to sing 'Don't Give It Up' at a show at The Roxy in Los Angeles – recorded for home-video and eventually released on CD. Other guests at the concert included Bob Weston, Mick Fleetwood and most of the current Fleetwood Mac lineup. The setlist mixed Welch's solo work with Fleetwood Mac songs from various periods. Proximity no longer seemed to pose a problem for Fleetwood and Weston – time and the dissolution of his marriage to Jenny having presumably diminished any animosity about Weston's affair with her.

The one then-current member of Fleetwood Mac who didn't appear at the show with Bob Welch, was Lindsey Buckingham, who'd recently released his own solo album. Solo was the operative term for the record, which he started working on at home – before Fleetwood Mac gathered to record basic tracks for their next album in May 1981 – and finished in a studio afterwards. Aside from a few key contributions from others, Buckingham sung and played nearly everything on *Law and Order* himself. Interviewed for a 1982 article in *People* magazine, he likened this process to that of a painter, in contrast to working with Fleetwood Mac: which he saw as 'more like making a movie.' Nevertheless, *Rolling Stone* and other publications perceived *Law and Order* as a continuation of his musical approach on *Tusk*. This is true to the extent that both records featured him playing around with the pop song format, though *Law and*

Order adopted a decidedly retro approach. In a press release for the album, Buckingham said one of his goals was 'to achieve a throwback sound, a rejection of 1981 'state of the art,' in favor of a sound maybe less correct technically, but far richer aesthetically.' Arguably, he undersold his achievement in the former area, but largely achieved it in the latter, creating a unique fusion between pre-Beatles rock-and-roll and new wave song styles. While *Law and Order* only reached 32 in the US, the success of the single 'Trouble' gave Buckingham credibility as a performer in his own right.

Law and Order – Lindsey Buckingham (1981)

Personnel:
Lindsey Buckingham: vocals, guitar, bass, keyboards, drums, percussion
Mick Fleetwood: drums ('Trouble')
George Hawkins: bass ('Trouble')
Carol Ann Harris: backing vocals ('It Was I')
Christine McVie: backing vocals ('Shadow Of The West')
Producers: Lindsey Buckingham, Richard Dashut
Release date: 3 October 1981
Chart places: US: 32, UK: -
Running Time: 36:31
All songs written by Lindsey Buckingham, except where noted.
Side One: 1. 'Bwana', 2. 'Trouble', 3. 'Mary Lee Jones', 4. 'I'll Tell You Now', 5. 'It Was I' (Gary Paxton)
Side Two: 1. 'September Song' (Kurt Weill, Maxwell Anderson), 2. 'Shadow Of The West', 3. 'That's How We Do It in L.A.', 4. 'Johnny Stew', 5. 'Love From Here, Love From There', 6. 'A Satisfied Mind' (Jack Rhodes, Red Hayes)

In contrast to Stevie Nicks, who took great pride in her songwriting ability, Lindsey Buckingham considered himself more of 'a musical stylist.' Consequently, Buckingham's songwriting doesn't lend itself to biographical assessments to the same degree his former partner's material does. That said, some people have interpreted the *Law and Order* opening track – the somewhat outlandish 'Bwana' – as a commentary of some sort about Mick Fleetwood's *The Visitor*. Buckingham subtitling the song 'The Visitor' for its single release, and using that phrase throughout the lyric, lends itself to that interpretation. However, anyone looking for insight into his mindset would probably gravitate to the line, 'We all have our demons, and sometimes they escape.' That line was a late addition to the song, which came about when co-producer Richard Dashut suggested Buckingham try singing the lead vocal for the largely finished track in the style of doo-wop singer Frankie Lymon (best known for 'Why Do Fools Fall in Love'). Doing so, he found that 'in a matter of minutes, a whole new melody and set of words emerged.'

If those words were somehow about Mick Fleetwood, it's unlikely anything untoward was intended. Since Dashut didn't come on board as co-producer until after the sessions with Fleetwood Mac, the reworking of 'Bwana' would've occurred after Fleetwood played his recording of 'Walk A Thin Line' to Buckingham. Fleetwood's account of Buckingham's appreciation for that musical gesture seems incongruous with any negative intent on the guitarist's part.

Supposition about lyrics aside, Fleetwood still had a tangible role on the album – playing drums on its most famous song: 'Trouble'. What ended up on the record, though, took a slightly different form. Buckingham recalled: '(Mick) came in one night, and we stayed till four in the morning doing takes. But when we came in the next day, there wasn't one take we felt was solid enough from start to finish. So we decided to cut a short tape loop of the drum track: only four seconds, I think.' He then overdubbed cymbals and fills to create the finished track.

The irony of using overdubbing to give the record a live feel, was not lost on him, but was also beside the point. Buckingham conceded in interviews that 'Trouble' was a rare case where he'd written a good melody, and his handling of the song emphasized its strengths. Along with strong vocal harmonies, he added a graceful Spanish guitar solo, and this combination of elements sounded great on the radio all around the world. The song reached the top 10 in the US and Canada, topped the singles charts in Australia and South Africa, and hit the Top 40 in the UK and other countries.

More recently, in a Q&A for the publication *Stereogum*, Buckingham commented that because he undertook *Law and Order* in the wake of *Tusk* being rejected on multiple fronts, the resulting album was 'sarcastic as a body of work.' 'Trouble' was a notable exception, which he identified as part of his rationale for releasing it as a single – a move that put him prominently on display on the recently-launched US cable channel MTV. The simple performance video – augmented by its own forms of technical trickery – was a low-budget affair compared to some later videos by Fleetwood Mac and its other members, but it suits the song.

Though he doesn't see songwriting as his strong point, Lindsey Buckingham's compositions still convey a great deal more emotional sincerity than he credits them with, as shown by the album's next two songs. 'Mary Lee Jones' and 'I'll Tell You Now' are very different from each other in tone, but both depict doubt and sadness. While 'Mary Lee Jones' offers a more upbeat surface, 'I'll Tell You Now' leans into a reflective mood that Buckingham framed as, 'The feeling of needing to communicate, but not having the emotional momentum to do so.'

> I felt the same today
> The same as always
> I guess you must wonder why
> I'll tell you, tell you now

'I'll Tell You Now' also provides an example of how porous the boundaries could be between the individual Fleetwood Mac members' solo work and their group efforts. According to Buckingham, 'Had (the song) been written a few months earlier, it probably would've gone on the *Tusk* album.'

That thread of sincerity carries through to the album's three songs *not* composed by Buckingham. The other aspect that stands out about these cover versions is how well his interpretations fit his stylistic choices for the album. The first of them – 'It Was I' – was originally recorded in 1959 and became a hit for the duo Skip and Flip. 'Flip' was a stage name for the song's writer Gary S. Paxton. While Skip and Flip didn't last, Paxton continued to work in music, producing the novelty hit 'Monster Mash', among others. After converting to Christianity, he worked in gospel music – a development that led to him becoming a character in the Oscar-nominated movie *The Eyes of Tammy Faye*. While Buckingham described the original recording as sounding amateurish – perhaps referring to the almost anonymous sound of the performances – the song had stuck with him since hearing it when he was younger. His version wasn't just more polished, it emphasized the inherent drama of the song's scenario, turning a good breakup song into a great one. Unfortunately, when released as a single, 'It Was I' didn't match the performance of the 1959 version, let alone 'Trouble'.

Side Two of *Law and Order* opened with 'September Song': a 1938 pop standard composed by Kurt Weill and Maxwell Anderson. Recorded numerous times by artists ranging from Frank Sinatra to Lou Reed,

Buckingham talked about wanting to record it for several years before this album, but didn't know the words. Help came in the form of his late father's collection of 78 records:

> When my father died several years ago, he left an extensive collection of 78s dating back to the 1920s, and last Christmas I finally got around to picking them up from my mother's house in Northern California. The collection was quite influential on many songs on the album. There happened to be a Frank Sinatra 78 of 'September Song' in there, and that's where I got the words. This is obviously another song with '40s flavor, but rocked up a tad.

The musical callbacks continued with 'Shadow Of The West' – a song written in the style of the old-time singing group Sons of the Pioneers – featuring vocal harmonies from Christine McVie. Buckingham explained: 'It's about having to deal with loss. Loss of time, loss of memories, love, youth.'

> Once upon a time I was strong and proud
> Everything that the law would allow
> But more and more I feel less and less
> I'm a shadow shadow shadow of the west

'Can you imagine how the atmosphere of '50s rock 'n' roll would suffer if it had to be recorded under today's so-called *perfect* conditions?' That rhetorical question posed in the *Law and Order* press release was in reference to 'That's How We Do It in L.A.' With its almost circular lyrics and jumpy rhythm, Buckingham saw it akin to the approach of rock music pioneers like Little Richard, Fats Domino and Jerry Lee Lewis: 'People seem to think the song is gonzo, but it's no more so than many rock 'n' roll songs from 25 years ago.'

If any song from *Law and Order* is sufficiently unusual to qualify as 'gonzo', 'Johnny Stew' takes the prize, with its attempts to imitate the sound of horns on guitar, and an unexpected mid-song interlude. The song title refers to the nickname for singer-songwriter John Stewart. Stewart – who first came to prominence as a member of the folk group The Kingston trio, and later as a songwriter (composing The Monkees' hit 'Daydream Believer') – was an early musical influence on Buckingham, to whom Stewart paid his own musical tribute with a song called 'Liddy Buck'. Buckingham returned the favor by producing Stewart's 1979 album *Bombs Away Dream Babies* (which featured the hit single 'Gold'), and appearing in a TV special celebrating The Kingston Trio, which aired in the US on the PBS network in 1982.

Stewart was also an influence on this song's lyric, which Buckingham came up with while joking around with Stewart in the studio. Among other things, they reference The Kingston Trio's interpretation of the traditional song 'Worried Man Blues.'

It takes a worried man now to sing a worried song
Johnny, oh Johnny, I know you were not wrong

The last Buckingham song on the album is the jaunty 'Love From Here, Love From There': another song for which his father's record collection provided a springboard. In this Dixieland-inspired piece, he uses guitars to fill the parts of the arrangement that would typically be played by wind instruments. Meanwhile, the lyric finds him upbeat but also a bit philosophical.

With love from here, love from there
You only get one bite

Law and Order closes with another standard. The list of artists who've recorded Red Hayes and Jack Rhodes' 'A Satisfied Mind' includes Ella Fitzgerald, Jonathan Richman and a variety of country artists. Buckingham again drew from the library of songs his father loved, and put his own spin on Red and Betty Foley's famous rendition: a country hit from 1955. As a successful but troubled rock star, Buckingham doubtless related to the lyric in a different way than most listeners.

The wealthiest person is a pauper at times
Compared to the man with a satisfied mind

With the initial wave of solo projects completed, the members of Fleetwood Mac devoted their collective energies to finishing their next endeavor as a group. Though not the last record released by this lineup, *Mirage* largely closed the book on these five musicians as a band that worked collaboratively.

Left: Despite viewing *Bella Donna* as an outlet for her own songs, Nicks made an exception for one artist – Tom Petty.

Right: Co-written by Petty, 'Stop Draggin' My Heart Around' became both artists' biggest hit.

Left: The music video for 1982's 'Hold Me' evoked the work of surrealist painter Rene Magritte.

Right and below: Though written by Christine McVie, 'Hold Me' was effectively a duet with Lindsey Buckingham.

Left: Filmed in the Mojave Desert, the 'Hold Me' video never shows the entire band together.

Ultimate Soft

Right: Nevertheless, the success of the song made the veteran band mainstays on the recently launched MTV.

Left and below: Lindsey Buckingham's Buddy Holly-influenced track 'Oh Diane' was released as the third single from *Mirage* in the UK.

Right: When it became a top ten hit there, Fleetwood Mac appeared on the BBC's long-running program *Top of the Pops.*

Left: Their mimed performance was an atypical pop-star moment within the band setting for Buckingham.

1982: If You Ever Want To Be There

The history of Fleetwood Mac is full of milestones that substantiate the saying that context is everything. For almost any other band, a record with songs and performances as strong as those on 1982's *Mirage* would've been recognized as an unqualified triumph. Instead – though stylistically closer to their self-titled 1975 album or *Rumours* – Mirage, rather than *Tusk*, is the outlier among this incarnation of Fleetwood Mac's recorded work: a remarkably strange status for a multi-platinum album containing some of the band's biggest US and UK hits.

Officially, Mick Fleetwood was no longer the band's manager, but he still had considerable influence on their direction. Writing in his first autobiography, he acknowledged that *Mirage* was, 'an attempt to get into the *Rumours* groove again.'

As with *Rumours*, the group decided to hold the initial recording sessions away from Los Angeles in order to sidestep distractions. Combined with a desire to help Mick address his financial issues, this led them much further afield than Sausalito, where they recorded much of the earlier album. Since Fleetwood had recently become a citizen of Monte Carlo, recording the album outside the US lessened his tax liability there. The band chose a location brimming with history: Le Chateau d'Hérouville. Located near Paris, the 18th-century house had been used as a recording studio since 1969, and had already claimed its place in popular-music history by the time Fleetwood Mac arrived in spring 1981. Among its many previous residents was Elton John, who recorded three albums there, including one that alluded to the studio in its title: 1972's *Honky Chateau*.

The band found Le Chateau to be a very different environment than they were used to. Christine McVie told Rolling Stone in 2016: 'It was extremely odd in the sense that it wasn't really a studio. It really was a rather beaten-up old castle. We were living in it, and then there was another area that was made to be a studio.' Nevertheless, the house offered a unique atmosphere. 'There was supposedly a ghost, and I was, of course, a sucker for the company,' Fleetwood commented in the *Mirage* liner notes – a sentiment echoed by Stevie Nicks: 'They thought it might be haunted because there were strange sounds in there. The place felt like the setting for an old movie murder-mystery ... There was one day when Jimmy Iovine – who I'd been dating and came to visit me – *did* want to kill Lindsey.'

Christine McVie recalled the recording sessions being largely free of acrimony. However, past or present romantic entanglements weren't the main impediment to renewed cohesion. Lindsey said, 'Mick used to have these broad-strokes ideas, and I think that going to France was an attempt to recreate an environment that was exotic and away from home, as we had with Rumours.' Fleetwood's drive to get 'more of a representation of the whole band, and perhaps more of what people who loved the band, wanted' was well-intentioned and understandable.

For many bands, a back-to-basics album is a means to reaffirm their musical identity. But for better or worse, Fleetwood Mac was beyond the point where Mick's conscious effort to recapture 'that same sort of drama and sense of theatre that had worked for us before' was likely to succeed. As Buckingham saw it, 'The attempt to *create* that kind of spontaneity, to me, spoke of the fact that he was trying to create a moment in time that had come and gone. But I tried to do what I could.' While the guitarist was also well-intentioned, that didn't make the process easy for him after the experimentation he'd been able to pursue on both *Tusk* and his own album. He admitted in 2016: 'It was hard to know where to go at that moment when you had just gone somewhere in one direction that felt right. Then to have to sort of reel it back in a more-forced way, felt difficult.' This echoed comments he made in 1982:

This time I wanted all my songs to be *band* songs, and the result of that, is an album that is a little less bizarre. *Tusk* had things that were good artistically, but it wasn't good for the whole band, and I thought that I should limit that to my solo albums. If I want to be in a band, we should play as a band, and maybe the result of that is that *Mirage* is a little more traditional in some senses.

Christine McVie's assessment was more pointed. In a 2003 piece for *Uncut* magazine, she observed, '*Mirage* was an attempt to get back into the flow that *Rumours* had. But we missed a vital ingredient: that was the passion.' Her view is understandable but also an overstatement. While *Mirage*'s immaculately-crafted portraits of relationships in flux and love gone wrong come across as more wistful than bitter, the record doesn't lack feeling. Likewise, Buckingham reining in his sonic experiments, didn't necessitate a lack of invention in the playing or production. McVie observed in a 1982 piece: 'I don't really imagine anybody else being able to do what he does with my songs.'

In some respects, the guitarist's contributions on *Mirage* are more impressive because they elevate the material without being overwhelming, as sometimes happened on *Tusk*. In Buckingham's compositions – and those of McVie and Nicks – an underlying simplicity welcomes the instrumental sparkle he brings. Listened to alongside *Tusk* and *Law and Order*, *Mirage* is a reminder that divisions between pre-Beatles rock and post-punk were more about attitude than actuality. If it feels less essential than *Rumours* or *Tusk*, *Mirage* is nevertheless the sound of Fleetwood Mac at their most fundamental – an album where they created excellent music, not because of emotional turmoil or to prove a point about their relevance, but simply because it's what they do. By that measure, it's as strong a testimony to their talent as either of the more-respected albums that preceded it.

Though Fleetwood Mac tended to be their own harshest critics, reviewers also had their say on the record. Reviews were generally positive, yet almost grudgingly so. Outlets such as *Esquire* praised the record as a return to form after several alternately self-indulgent and eccentric group and solo efforts, while other critics walked the thin line of acknowledging the album's virtues while still conveying that they found something to be lacking. *Village Voice* critic Robert Christgau exemplified the latter, having found himself 'alternately charmed by its craft, and offended by its banality.'

Whatever disquiet Fleetwood Mac themselves or outside critics felt about the work, fans didn't hesitate to embrace it. *Mirage* quickly reached five in the UK, and it became Fleetwood Mac's third chart-topping album in the US.

Mirage (1982)

Personnel:
Lindsey Buckingham: guitar, vocals, additional keyboards
Mick Fleetwood: drums, percussion
Christine McVie: keyboards, vocals
John McVie: bass
Stevie Nicks: vocals
Additional personnel:
Ray Lindsey: additional guitar on 'Straight Back'
Producers: Lindsey Buckingham, Richard Dashut, Ken Caillat, Fleetwood Mac
Engineers: Ken Caillat, Richard Dashut, Carla Frederick, Dennis Mays, David Bianco, Sabrina Buchanek, Boa

Release date: 18 June 1982
Chart places: US: 1, UK: 5
Running Time: 42:52 (original release)
Side One: 1. 'Love In Store' (Christine McVie, John Recor), 2. 'Can't Go Back' (Buckingham), 3. 'That's Alright' (Nicks), 4. 'Book Of Love' (Buckingham, Dashut), 5. 'Gypsy' (Nicks), 6. 'Only Over You' (McVie)
Side Two: 1. 'Empire State' (Buckingham, Dashut), 2. 'Straight Back' (Nicks), 3. 'Hold Me' (McVie, Robbie Patton), 4. 'Oh Diane' (Buckingham, Dashut), 5. 'Eyes Of The World' (Buckingham), 6. 'Wish You Were Here' (McVie, Colin Allen)
2016 Deluxe Edition Disc Two – B-sides, Outtakes, Sessions
1. 'Love In Store' (Early version) (McVie, Recor), 2. 'Suma's Walk aka Can't Go Back' (Outtake) (Buckingham), 3. 'That's Alright' (Alternate take) (Nicks), 4. 'Book Of Love' (Early version) (Buckingham, Dashut), 5. 'Gypsy' (Early version) (Nicks), 6. 'Only Over You' (McVie), 7. 'Empire State' (Early version) (Buckingham, Dashut), 8. 'If You Were My Love' (Outtake) (Nicks), 9. 'Hold Me' (Early version) (McVie, Patton), 10. 'Oh Diane' (Early Version) (Buckingham, Dashut), 11. 'Smile At You' (Outtake) (Nicks), 12. 'Goodbye Angel' (Original outtake) (Buckingham), 13. 'Eyes Of The World' (Alternate early version) (Buckingham), 14. 'Straight Back' (Original vinyl version) (Nicks), 15. 'Wish You Were Here' (Alternate version) (McVie, Allen), 16. 'Cool Water' (Bob Nolan), 17. 'Gypsy' (Video version) (Nicks), 18. 'Put A Candle In The Window' (Run-through) (McVie), 19. 'Teen Beat' (Outtake) (Buckingham, Dashut), 20. 'Blue Monday' (Jam) (Dave Bartholomew)
2016 Deluxe Edition Disc Three – Live at The Forum, Los Angeles, California 21-22 October 1982: 1. 'The Chain' (Fleetwood Mac), 2. 'Gypsy' (Nicks), 3. 'Love In Store' (McVie, Recor), 4. 'Not That Funny' (Buckingham), 5. 'You Make Loving Fun' (McVie), 6. 'I'm So Afraid' (Buckingham), 7. 'Blue Letter' (Richard Curtis, Michael Curtis), 8. 'Rhiannon' (Nicks), 9. 'Tusk' (Buckingham), 10. 'Eyes Of The World' (Buckingham), 11. 'Go Your Own Way' (Buckingham), 12. 'Sisters Of The Moon' (Nicks), 13. 'Songbird' (McVie)

While it seems strange to say about a record as unassuming as *Mirage*, Christine McVie's upbeat 'Love In Store' serves as a statement-of-purpose. Lyrically it sings the praises of a new relationship. But many fans could also see it as a reflection of their own feelings about the band.

All I know is the way that I feel
Whenever you're around
You've got a way of lifting me up
Instead of bringing me down

Musically, the mid-tempo piece is enlivened by Nicks and Buckingham's backing vocals, which call to mind the pre-Beatles stylings the latter explored on *Law and Order*. Though not one of their bigger hits, 'Love In Store' is noteworthy for being McVie's first Fleetwood Mac song co-written with someone outside of the band. Her co-writer Jim Recor – ex-husband of Mick Fleetwood's then-current partner Sara Recor – added a certain soap-opera aspect.

But 'Love In Store' wasn't McVie's only *Mirage* song written with an outside writer. Nor was she the only band member who worked with others on the majority of her contributions. While the album was intended to showcase Fleetwood Mac as a unit, half the songs were written with people outside the band, including three of Buckingham's, which he wrote with Richard Dashut. The second track, 'Can't Go Back', was one of the two he composed alone. A melody and accompaniment as upbeat as 'Love In Store,' counterpoint the pensive lyric.

Melodies awaken sorrows from their sleep
I wanna go back

That thread of melancholy continues with Nicks' 'That's Alright.' Of the band's three writers, she was the only one to write all her *Mirage* songs solo. The country-inflected 'That's Alright' was one she'd written a decade earlier, before she and Buckingham moved to Los Angeles. It might not have been as premonitory as the same period's 'After The Glitter Fades,' but lyrics like 'I decided yesterday that I would leave you' are a tuneful reminder that the tensions between the pair *preceded* them joining Fleetwood Mac.

Buckingham's 1950s inspirations show through again on the decidedly retro 'Book Of Love', which makes a companion piece to his cover of 'It Was I.' One of the harsher critiques in *Rolling Stone*'s *Mirage* review was John Milward's assessment of the disconnect between the quality of Buckingham's melodies and lyrics recycled from older songs. Noting that 'Who wrote the book of love?' was far from an original line, is true enough. However, Milward missed the point when asserting that, 'While Buddy Holly, Eddie Cochran and Brian Wilson fire his imagination, they also tangle his tongue.'

The latter comment ignored both the extent to which Buckingham consciously chose to embrace this style, and the skill he displayed in making it his own.

In silence the lonely make all their mistakes
Tore a page of my heart

The guitarist isn't credited as a composer on the next song, but he played a key role in making it the album's most iconic track. According to various accounts – including that in Mick Fleetwood's second autobiography – Stevie Nicks wrote 'Gypsy' for *Bella Donna*, but saved it for the band. Fleetwood described it as 'a perfect portrait of the people we were at the dawn of the 1980s. It has a wise, world-weary melancholy that's as poignant as anything off *Rumours*.' Christine McVie unequivocally labeled it as the album's best track, telling *Rolling Stone* in 2016: 'It's very musical. Very melodic. All the parts are right. It's just a very beautiful record.' That comment speaks to Buckingham's contribution to the track, which he discussed in a 2003 piece in *Performing Songwriter*:

Maybe that's my favorite example of it coming together. If you sing, 'You see your gypsy, you see your gypsy, yeah,' it doesn't really depart anywhere at the point it needs to. It just sounds like someone jamming with their voice, but it allows the openness for me to do the things of my own. It's a real collaboration, even though I'm not writing the song.

Another factor in the song's popularity is its memorable music video. 'I know the record company spent a lot of money on it', said Christine McVie, alluding to its reputation as the most expensive music video made up to that point. Though the cult-classic *Highlander* movie was still a few years in his future, director Russell Mulcahy was well-established in music videos, having made the first one to be played on MTV: The Buggles' 'Video Killed The Radio Star', and many others. The video's understandable focus on Stevie Nicks, might not have helped the band's internal dynamics, but it did something relatively few manage. Amid the elegant evocation of old-Hollywood glamor, it keeps the focus on the song and its glorious reminiscence of the singer's pre-stardom life.

To the gypsy that remains
Faces freedom with a little fear
I have no fear
I have only love

'Gypsy' also became a tribute to Nicks' best friend from high school: Robin Snyder Anderson. Anderson – who'd become a much-loved part of Fleetwood Mac's extended family – was diagnosed with leukemia around the time of *Bella Donna*, and lost her battle with the disease soon after the release of *Mirage*.

Based on the credit 'Special thanks for inspiration to Dennis Wilson,' the inspiration for Christine McVie's 'Only Over You' was relatively recent. Her relationship with Wilson had ended before the recording sessions for *Mirage* began, but the ballad's earnest lyric reflects the great affection she had for him while they were together.

> People say they know me
> But they don't see
> My heart's your future
> Your future is me

Though love songs had been the backbone of Fleetwood Mac's recent albums, the band's other writers occasionally explored other subjects. For her part, McVie preferred to stick to her strength. She commented in a 2004 article in UK magazine *The Word*: 'I can't do heavy messages in music. I've tried and never even recorded them. I write relationship songs. I just don't know how to do anything else.'

Side two starts with an example of Buckingham reconciling his drive to find new sounds with the expectations surrounding the band. Another collaboration with Richard Dashut, the impressionistic 'Empire State' is the album's closest thing to Buckingham's less-conventional *Tusk* pieces. However, rather than rough edges snagging, the song glides along, thanks to an effortless groove from Mick Fleetwood and John McVie, with Buckingham's distinctive guitar figure and lyrics cementing its upbeat mood.

> Big Apple takin' a bite of me
> Whole world movin' below my feet
> Not like, not like we do in L.A.

Stevie Nicks' displays her own stylistic evolution on 'Straight Back,' which was virtually the polar opposite of 'That's Alright.' Where 'That's Alright' sounded like a cousin of earlier songs like 'Landslide', the keyboard-based arrangement of 'Straight Back' prefigured some of the more-synthesizer-oriented tracks on Nicks' next solo album. Despite the emphasis on synthesizers, her vocals are no less impassioned, though the lyric feels alternately concrete and opaque – not just in the refrain 'The dream has just begun,' but throughout the verses.

She remembers how good it can be
He remembers a melody
Ah, in the shadow of my shadow
In a gleam

While many fans probably associate the album's biggest US hit 'Hold Me' more with the desert-set music video that evoked surrealist Rene Margritte, it was another song rooted in Christine McVie's tumultuous relationship with Dennis Wilson. In a 2004 interview with journalist Robin Eggar, McVie recalled: 'It was an unlikely relationship. Opposites attract, I suppose. I found him insane. Because of that, I found him very attractive.' As troubled as his brother Brian – just in different ways – Wilson's propensity to overindulge in drugs, alcohol and female companionship was widely known: certainly to Mick Fleetwood, who introduced Wilson to McVie. Fleetwood wrote: 'I was very torn, because Dennis was a friend, and I'd see him fucking up and chasing skirts, and didn't know whether it was my role to say anything to Chris. In the end, I didn't have to.'

I don't want no damage
How'm I gonna manage with you
You hold the percentage
But I'm the fool payin' the dues

'Hold Me' is effectively a duet between McVie and Buckingham – an aspect with roots in the song's composition, which was a joint effort between McVie and Robbie Patton. McVie later told *Rolling Stone*: 'When I wrote the song with Robbie, he was also a singer, and he was always singing a lower part. And so, at some point, it became obvious to me that Lindsey would eventually do it.'

The vocal duet is mirrored by the instrumental interplay between McVie on piano, and Buckingham's multilayered guitar work, which includes one of his most distinctive Fleetwood Mac solos. Like most of the album's songs, 'Hold Me' has an alternative version that's included on the 2016 deluxe edition. These early versions and alternate takes show the songs to be fully-formed while giving a window into how adjustments to vocals and accompaniment, shaped the songs. In the case of 'Hold Me,' the early takes' rough edges reveal a familial affinity with the *Tusk* song 'Think About Me.'

The comparison with Buddy Holly's band The Crickets that Robert A. Hull made when reviewing Fleetwood Mac's 1980 live album, seems especially apt when listening to 'Oh Diane.' The surprisingly-sweet song – the third Buckingham/Dashut co-write – can be seen as Lindsey's answer to the Buddy Holly song 'Peggy Sue.' The lyric isn't especially deep, but combined with the breezy melody, it helped make the song a top-10 hit in the UK.

Love is like a grain of sand
Slowly slippin' through your hand

If not necessarily deeper than 'Oh Diane', 'Eyes Of The World' feels more substantial. The repeated refrain 'Back and forth lies unfurl/In the eyes, in the eyes, in the eyes of the world' is matched by the drive of Fleetwood and John McVie, and also Buckingham's guitar work. He played the song in 1992 on his first solo tour, and it's one of the few *Mirage* songs that Fleetwood Mac has performed in concert since 1982.

Christine McVie gets the album's last word – one in keeping with the strand of melancholy that pervades the album. Written with Colin Allen (another former drummer for John Mayall and the Bluesbreakers), the album-closer 'Wish You Were Here' is a musical cousin of previous McVie showcases like 'Songbird.' Though Fleetwood Mac never played the song in concert, McVie rated it highly enough to add it to the setlist of her joint 2017 tour with Lindsey Buckingham.

Rain on my window
I can count the drops
But I can't help feeling lonely
There's no way that I can stop

The recent vogue for alternate versions of well-known albums, sometimes gets in the way of appreciating the original records' merits. Conversely, the combination of alternate versions and outtakes for *Mirage* demonstrate that whatever equivocations they felt compelled to offer after the fact,

Fleetwood Mac made the record they set out to. On balance, the early versions of most of the album's tracks are a tribute to their craftsmanship and the band's understanding of how to finesse their work. As for the outtakes, they demonstrate how song-selection impacted the album as much as the manner in which those songs were recorded. This is less obvious with the Buckngham and McVie songs. Had *Mirage* been released in the CD era when album running times became more flexible, the yearning 'Goodbye Angel' and the mid-tempo rocker 'Put A Candle In The Window' would both have meshed well with the album's overall feel.

Stevie Nicks' non-album songs are a different matter. She wrote and recorded 'If You Were My Love' while working on *Bella Donna*, though the version she made with Fleetwood Mac had a harder sound than the one produced by Jimmy Iovine. 'Smile At You' dated back to 1976 and displayed a similar edge to Nicks' cathartic *Rumours* outtake 'Silver Springs.' She told Blair Jackson in 1981: 'I think Lindsey wants me to record another one, and so do I. It's kind of a bitter song, and that's really not where any of us are right now, even though it's a wonderful song.'

What you did not need was a lady who was stronger
You needed someone to depend on you
Well I could not be her
But I did not want to
My first mistake was to smile at you

Nicks was right about 'Smile At You', and 'If You Were My Love' was also a fine song. *Mirage* just wasn't the right setting for them. She revisited 'Smile At You' in a less-impassioned form on a later Fleetwood Mac album and eventually re-recorded 'If You Were My Love' for *24 Karat Gold: Songs from the Vault*: her 2014 collection devoted to previously-unreleased songs.

Shortly after the release of *Mirage*, the band prepared to tour again. For better or worse, this was a much shorter run than the *Tusk* tour, focusing on the United States and lasting less than two months. A 1982 article with the eye-catching title 'Where's Stevie?' in US magazine *Record*, pointed to the fault lines within the band leading into the tour. McVie said Stevie 'asks what songs we plan on doing and what songs we want her to do. The rest of it will be decided between Mick, Lindsey and me.'

Despite its brevity, the tour included some noteworthy dates. On 5 September, the band headlined the final day of the US Festival in

California – a multi-day event organized by Apple co-founder Steve Wozniak and legendary concert promoter Bill Graham. The festival had the laudable aim of fostering increased community in the wake of the *me decade*, and had a lineup including some of the world's most popular bands. And even after losing millions of dollars, Wozniak decided to hold another the following year.

The band's October shows at the Los Angeles venue The Forum, were recorded for a concert special that aired on HBO. That program was later released on home-video, with the audio portion becoming the third disc of the 2016 deluxe edition of *Mirage*.

A show a few days earlier, held greater significance. On 5 October, Robin Anderson succumbed to her illness after delivering her son Matthew via an emergency Caesarean section with Stevie Nicks becoming the boy's godmother. Struck by Anderson's death both individually and collectively, Fleetwood Mac played a benefit concert on 18 October to raise money for City of Hope: a Los Angeles hospital known for being a cancer-treatment center. Glenn Frey opened the show with a set featuring guest appearances from Boz Scaggs and Joe Walsh, and Frey's former bandmate Don Henley joined Fleetwood Mac to reprise his duet 'Leather And Lace' with Stevie Nicks.

While the band members continued working on their solo projects, live performances outside the band were infrequent in 1982. Buckingham was the musical guest on a February episode of *Saturday Night Live*, playing 'Trouble' and 'Bwana', backed by Mick Fleetwood and some of the musicians who became part of the drummer's auxiliary band The Zoo. In June, Stevie Nicks performed at Peace Sunday – a concert promoting nuclear disarmament, held at the Rose Bowl stadium in Pasadena, California. The impressive lineup also included Jackson Browne, Stevie Wonder and Joan Baez. Along with a short solo set that mixed 'Edge Of Seventeen' with Fleetwood Mac material, Nicks joined other acts for the closing numbers: Crosby, Stills & Nash's 'Teach Your Children' and John Lennon's 'Give Peace A Chance.'

There would be five years and just as many solo albums between *Mirage* and the next Fleetwood Mac album. Some were more successful than others, but each was noteworthy for embodying the individual members' contribution to the group's sound while inspiring questions about its future. Drama remained a constant for the band members – just not on an ensemble basis, for the moment.

Right: Fleetwood Mac's October 1982 shows at The Forum in Los Angeles were recorded for a concert film on HBO.

Left: Stevie Nicks' second solo album, 1983's *The Wild Heart*, solidified Stevie Nicks' stature as a solo artist. (*Modern*)

Right: *I'm Not Me* by Mick Fleetwood's Zoo is the most underrated Fleetwood Mac solo project of the 1980s. (*RCA*)

1983: Read Between My Lines

When journalist Blair Jackson asked Lindsey Buckingham how Fleetwood Mac had avoided the appearance of being a 'corporate monolith' despite their immense success, the answer – like so many things with the band – involved *Rumours*: 'That might've added a human touch to the band, that still remains. Showing some of ourselves in a very honest and succinct way, might've affected the way people view the group as a whole.'

Even by the measure of her fellow songwriters in the band, the line between Stevie Nicks' music and her personal life, often seemed remarkably thin. This was part of her appeal within the band and as a solo performer. However, where the semi-democracy of a group provided checks and balances to keep any one member from artistic excess – *Tusk* notwithstanding – there were far fewer constraints on a solo artist: especially one whose first album had been as popular as *Bella Donna* was. In the same way that Fleetwood Mac in 1982 attempted with *Mirage* to reset their balance between artistic and commercial success, 1983 found Nicks looking to recapture the success of *Bella Donna*.

In both cases, though, the passage of time and a series of arduous events put their goals out of reach. Buckingham, in a 1982 article: 'Stevie has never been very happy, and I don't think the success of her album has made her any happier. In fact, it may have made her less happy.' Buckingham's contention is debatable, and certainly biased, but there's no question Nicks was consumed with sadness when she began work on her second solo album. She said in 2016: 'I remember turning into a ghost of regret. What was left, was just a big, horrible, empty world. Nothing was important to me when Robin died.' The singer's grief over Robin Anderson's death, came through in multiple songs on *The Wild Heart*, and had a powerful impact on her personal life. As the godmother of Robin's son Matthew, Stevie felt a need to ensure the boy was looked after, leading to one of her most impulsive albeit well-intentioned decisions in a decade filled with them. The January 1983 news that Stevie Nicks was marrying Robin's widower Kim Anderson, came as a shock to the other band members. 'We all knew it was too soon,' recalled Mick Fleetwood in his first autobiography, describing the marriage as, 'a dramatic gesture by two people bonded together only in misery.' Christine McVie, who attended the wedding ceremony with

Fleetwood, also found the marriage odd. She explained to *Rolling Stone* the following year: 'It didn't seem like crazy love to me. I didn't buy her a wedding present.' Nicks and Anderson soon recognized their mistake for themselves and divorced just a few months after the wedding. Nicks told *Us* magazine: 'We didn't get married because we were in love; we got married because we were grieving and it was the only way that we could feel like we were doing anything.' Nicks didn't see Matthew for many years after the divorce, but they eventually reconnected.

The brief marriage to Kim Anderson coincided with the dissolution of another romantic relationship for Nicks. She recounted for a 2007 article in *Performing Songwriter*: 'During *Wild Heart,* I was coming to the end of my relationship with Jimmy Iovine, so that was really hard. I had already gone through the whole Lindsey-and-Stevie thing, and now here I was back in another situation where I was working with somebody that I had loved and the relationship had started to fall apart.' Though it wasn't the only factor, Nicks acknowledged the impact of her drug use: 'Jimmy was not a drug user or a drinker, and the whole world was turning into a bunch of drug addicts at that point.'

Atlantic Records president Doug Morris – who helped connect Nicks and Iovine for the making of *Bella Donna* – remembered that their 'relationship did start to fray, and eventually ended, so there was a lot of fighting and disagreements. But they're both professionals and they worked through it.'

Whether judged creatively or commercially, sequels in any artistic medium are rarely as successful as their predecessors, and *The Wild Heart* was no exception. Along with Iovine, the album featured many of the same contributors that made *Bella Donna* a hit, including return appearances by Tom Petty and The Heartbreakers, and perhaps most importantly, her ubiquitous backing singers Sharon Celani and Lori Perry. Nicks said in 2016: 'The girls were my Fleetwood Mac. I wouldn't have a solo career without them. They were with me on all of it. I would've been so lonely being in a world of men making this record.'

However important the supporting cast was, the shortcomings of *The Wild Heart* largely stemmed from the star herself. Not so much Stevie Nicks the singer – who brought absolute commitment to the material – but rather Stevie Nicks the songwriter, whose compositions lacked the focus displayed on *Bella Donna. Rolling Stone* writer Christopher Connelly's July-1983 review was full of hyperbole, with the comment 'Much of *The Wild Heart* is an outright catastrophe' the most obvious.

But he rightly noted how a fairy-tale atmosphere made much of the album less compelling than it should be: 'Nicks gets distracted by the archetypal trappings – doves, gardens, beasts with hearts o' gold – and misses their emotional core. As a result, her lyrics are awash with setting, but curiously clumsy in matters of the heart.' Connelly wasn't the only critic to fault Nicks' writing. Nor was he the only one to acknowledge the strength of her singing, which seemed to be the element that mattered more to her fans.

The Wild Heart was another hit, certified Silver in the UK and Double-Platinum in the US, where it yielded three top 40 singles, and radio airplay for several other songs. What those songs reveal, is that the starkest contrast with the album's predecessor is that most of *The Wild Heart*'s best moments involve another writer's input.

The Wild Heart – Stevie Nicks (1983)

Personnel:
Side One:
1. 'Wild Heart' (Nicks)
Stevie Nicks: lead vocals, Sharon Celani, Lori Perry: backing vocals, Sandy Stewart: synthesizer, David Monday: guitar, Roger Tausz: bass, Brad Smith: drums, percussion, Dean Parks: guitar
2. 'If Anyone Falls' (Nicks, Sandy Stewart)
Stevie Nicks: lead vocals, Sharon Celani, Lori Perry: backing vocals, Russ Kunkel: drums, Roy Bittan: synthesizer, Waddy Wachtel: guitar, Bob Glaub: bass, Bobbye Hall: percussion, Carolyn Brooks: additional vocals
3. 'Gate And Garden' (Nicks)
Stevie Nicks: lead vocals, Sharon Celani, Lori Perry: backing vocals, Sandy Stewart: keyboards, synthesizer, David Monday: guitar, Brad Smith: drums, percussion, Waddy Wachtel: guitar, Benmont Tench: organ
4. 'Enchanted' (Nicks)
Stevie Nicks: lead vocals, Sharon Celani, Lori Perry: backing vocals, Russ Kunkel: drums, Waddy Wachtel: guitar, Bobbye Hall: percussion, Benmont Tench: organ, Roy Bittan: piano, Bob Glaub: bass
5. 'Nightbird' (Nicks, Stewart)
Stevie Nicks: lead vocals, Sharon Celani, Lori Perry: backing vocals, Kenny Edwards: bass, Waddy Wachtel: guitar, Benmont Tench: organ, Chet McCracken: drum overdubs, David Foster: piano, Marvin Caruso: drums, Sandy Stewart: synthesizer, vocals, piano solo, David Bluefield: drum machine programming

Side Two:

1. 'Stand Back' (Nicks)
Stevie Nicks: lead vocals, Sharon Celani, Lori Perry: backing vocals, David Williams: guitar, Sandy Stewart: synthesizer, Bobbye Hall: percussion, Waddy Wachtel: guitar, Ian Wallace: percussion, Russ Kunkel: drum overdubs, Steve Lukather: guitar, Marvin Caruso: drums, David Bluefield: drum machine programming, Prince: synthesizer (Uncredited)

2. 'I Will Run To You' (Tom Petty)
Stevie Nicks: lead vocals, Sharon Celani, Lori Perry: backing vocals, Tom Petty: guitar, vocals, Mike Campbell: guitar, Benmont Tench: keyboards, Stan Lynch: drums, Howie Epstein: bass

3. 'Nothing Ever Changes' (Nicks, Stewart)
Stevie Nicks: lead vocals, Sharon Celani, Lori Perry: backing vocals, Russ Kunkel: drums, Don Felder: guitar, Bob Glaub: bass, Roy Bittan: piano, Sandy Stewart: synthesizer, Phil Kenzie: saxophone, Bobbye Hall: percussion

4. 'Sable On Blond' (Nicks)
Stevie Nicks: lead vocals, Sharon Celani, Lori Perry: backing vocals, Mick Fleetwood: drums
Kenny Edwards: bass, Roy Bittan: piano, Waddy Wachtel: guitar, Sandy Stewart: synthesizer

5. 'Beauty And The Beast' (Nicks)
Stevie Nicks: lead vocals, Sharon Celani, Lori Perry: backing vocals, Roy Bittan: piano, John Beal: bass, Carolyn Brooks: additional vocals, Gene Bianco: harp, Jesse Levine, Julien Barber, Theodore Israel, Harry Zaratzian: viola, Jesse Levy, Frederick Zlotkin, Seymour Barbara, Jon Abramowitz: cello, Marvin Morgenstern, Herbert Sorkin, John Pintavalle, Max Ellen, Regis Eandiorio, Harry Glickman, Peter Dimitriades, Paul Winter, Matthew Raimondi, Harry Cykman, Raymond Kunicki, Lewis Eley, Ruth Waterman, Paul Gershman: violin
String arrangements: Paul Buckmaster, Kenneth Whitfield
Conductor: Paul Buckmaster

2016 Deluxe Edition Disc Two – Bonus Tracks
1. 'Violet And Blue' (from the Against All Odds soundtrack) (Nicks), 2. 'I Sing For The Things' (Unreleased version) (Nicks), 3. 'Sable On Blond' (Alternate version) (Nicks), 4. 'All The Beautiful Worlds' (Unreleased version) (Nicks), 5. 'Sorcerer' (Unreleased version) (Nicks), 6. 'Dial The Number' (Unreleased version) (Nicks, Stewart), 7. 'Garbo' (B-side) (Nicks), 8. 'Are You Mine' (Demo) (Nicks), 9. 'Wild Heart' (Session) (Nicks)
Original album producers: Jimmy Iovine, Gordon Perry ('Wild Heart', 'Gate and Garden'); Tom Petty ('I Will Run To You')

Engineers: Shelly Yakus, Greg Edward; Tom "Gordo" Gondolf ('Wild Heart',
'Gate and Garden')
Release date: 10 June 1983
Chart places: US: 5, UK: 28
Running time: 45:11 (Original release)

Like *Bella Donna*, *The Wild Heart* opens with its title track – a gesture
reflective of how Nicks saw the new album in relation to its *predecessor*:
'It's like *Bella Donna*'s heart is wild all of a sudden,' she commented in
Rock magazine. Later in the interview, she added, 'It's just *Bella Donna* a
little more reckless. She's just more sure of herself now, so she's taking
a few more chances.' Nicks referring to herself in character, points to
another difference with the album before. Where she saw Bella Donna
as presenting a chronology of her life, the world of *The Wild Heart* drew
as much from movies and personal mythology as it did from the singer's
real life: with the title song as a prime example. Initially inspired by
the 1939 movie *Wuthering Heights* and its ill-fated lovers Heathcliff and
Cathy, the song accrued further layers due to the events around Nicks, as
recounted in the liner notes for the album's 2016 reissue:

> I think 'Wild Heart' – as much as it was wholly inspired by the doomed
> romance of *Wuthering Heights* – is one of those songs that ended up
> about more than one thing. It's the same way 'Edge Of Seventeen'
> was about Tom Petty and his wife Jane, my uncle dying, and the
> assassination of John Lennon.

The additional preoccupations reflected in 'Wild Heart' included the
dichotomy between Nicks' abiding grief over Robin Anderson's death, and
the confidence she felt as an artist in her own right after the success of
Bella Donna. The former also found expression elsewhere on the album,
while the latter is particularly present here. 'I won the hearts of people
who also loved Fleetwood Mac, and certainly didn't want to quit the band.
But they were still really happy I'd made a solo record. So I was feeling a
lot more confident about going into a second solo album than I was when
I made *Bella Donna*.' That sentiment and a feeling that she could (arguably,
even should) take chances, found expression in the song's chorus.

> Don't blame it in me
> Blame it on my wild heart

Nicks declared: 'That was becoming my anthem after *Mirage* and *Bella Donna*. Basically, I was saying, 'Don't accuse me of anything, don't tell me what I can and cannot do, and don't blame it on me, blame it on my wild heart.'

Apart from Jimmy Iovine, Nicks' most important musical collaborator on *The Wild Heart* was singer-songwriter Sandy Stewart. Nicks commented in 1983: 'I've probably prayed for so many years that I'd find somebody I could write songs with, and I finally found her. She lives in Houston, and she's totally crazy; she's a real brilliant musician.'

Stewart, who Nicks met through singer Lori Perry's then-husband Gordon, played keyboards on six of the album's songs, and co-wrote three. The first of those – and according to Nicks, the first one she wrote 'in the same room' with someone – was 'If Anyone Falls.' The lyric has a fragmented quality, especially in the chorus:

If anyone falls in love
Somewhere, in the twilight, dreamtime
Somewhere, in the back of your mind
If anyone falls

Taken as a whole, the song has genuine presence, with an insistent rhythm and a catchy hook that helped it become a US top-20 hit. The hook largely stems from the keyboards – not by Sandy Stewart, but rather Roy Bittan: playing synthesizer here rather than his typical piano.

Stylistically, 'Gate And Garden' recalls the *Bella Donna* musical approach but also fits *The Wild Heart*'s default pattern of being musically direct but lyrically diffuse.

There is a gate
It can be guarded
Well, it is not heaven
And it has a garden
So to the red rose
Grows the passion

By her own admission, Stevie Nicks wasn't quite sure what the song was about, but still offered an interpretation in the press kit that accompanied the album's release: 'I guess it's my idea of escapes, of the places that I go, the things that I do and think about, that is my private, silent, secret garden world that belongs to nobody else.'

Based on its title alone, 'Enchanted' evokes the singer's mystical image, but is one of the album's more-straightforward rockers. This is fitting for the song's spontaneous origins. She described in the album's press kit: 'We wrote it last summer on the way from New York City to Quogue on Long Island. I mean, we wrote it in the car, in the limousine. We hooked up our TCD-5 (portable recorder), which is the saviour of our singing lives. So we sang and recorded, and by the time we got there, the song was written.' With lyrics like 'My destiny says that I'm destined to run,' the piano-driven track sounds like it was envisioned with the stage in mind, and made its live debut in one of the early shows of the tour for *The Wild Heart*. However, 'Enchanted' was quickly dropped from the setlist, and Nicks didn't start performing it with any regularity until the 1998 tour to promote her compilation of the same name.

On the surface, the atmosphere and sultry melody of 'Nightbird' leans into Nicks' siren-of-the-north image, with deliberate echoes of 'Edge Of Seventeen.' Like the album's title song, it's also rooted in her grief for Robin Anderson.

And when I call
Will you walk gently
Thru my shadow
The ones who sing at night

The catalyst for writing the song was an image from a collection of paintings and drawings by German artist Sulamith Wülfing, which Mick Fleetwood gave to Stevie shortly after she joined Fleetwood Mac. Nicks said in 2016: 'There's one called 'The Falling Leave,' with a girl looking up at a feather falling from the sky. That's what I was feeling about losing Robin.' While Nicks' recollection of the details is slightly off from the work itself (which features a leaf rather than a feather), it's easy to see how its mood inspired the words she turned into the album's strongest track, with help from Sandy Stewart: 'I said to Sandy that we had to do this together. She had to help me; the deadline was looming, but this song had to go on *The Wild Heart*. And she knew Robin, so she said, Okay! Your song, your words, and I'll try to work around you,' and Sandy did it.'

Side two of *The Wild Heart* begins with another co-write, though from a less-traditional method than 'Nightbird.' In addition to an atypical scenario, Nicks started writing 'Stand Back' while she and Kim Anderson were on their honeymoon. According to Nicks, it began with a song on the radio: 'I heard this wonderful song Prince had done called 'Little Red Corvette,' and as soon as I heard it, I went, 'Boy I love that,' and I just started humming to myself, and in a matter of minutes I'd hummed along a very different melody than what Prince had done.'

Putting the honeymoon aside, Anderson helped Nicks record a rough demo on a cassette recorder in their hotel room. Nicks shared her new song with Jimmy Iovine upon returning to Los Angeles. According to Iovine, the first attempt at recording 'Stand Back' at his studio, was lackluster. The initial recording 'sounded like a bunch of rock musicians making a club record. I said, 'Man, we need someone else in here.' Fittingly, the 'someone else' ended up being the song's *de facto* co-writer. Nicks called Prince, who came to the studio during a break from shooting a music video. Nicks recounted for the album's press kit: 'Under pressure of fire, we did it in one take, one time, and that's what you hear – me singing live, Sandy on her synthesizer, Prince playing that dahdahdahdahda very kind-of 'Edge Of Seventeen' thing and a drum machine.'

While Iovine described Prince's brief session appearance as 'extraordinary,' Nicks had a more-colorful recollection. She told James McNair in a 2013 *Mojo* interview: 'I remember him playing basketball outside, like one of the Harlem Globetrotters. He was spinning the ball on a finger and throwing it backwards into the net.' Nicks' friendship with Prince posed one of the more interesting what-ifs in pop-music history, when he asked her to write lyrics to the backing track for what eventually became 'Purple Rain.' She explained to McNair: 'I was overwhelmed. I told him, 'Prince, I've listened to this a hundred times, but I wouldn't know where to start. It's a movie, it's epic.' It *was* epic. And it *became* a movie.'

In its final form – including contributions from guitarists Steve Lukather and Waddy Wachtel – 'Stand Back' became one of Stevie's biggest solo hits, peaking at 5 in the US, and later becoming part of Fleetwood Mac's setlists: ''Stand Back' became a real anthem, a real 'I'm tired of listening to all your great advice, 'cause it's gotten me nowhere, so I'm listening to myself now' kind of anthem.'

So I walked down the line
Away from you
Maybe your attention was more
Than I could do

The genesis of 'Stand Back' embodies how *The Wild Heart* was governed more by Nicks' passions (and occasionally whims) than her artistic focus: a point echoed by the first of two music videos produced for the track. With imagery reminiscent of *Gone With the Wind*, the so-called 'Scarlett version' of 'Stand Back' was the singer's own concept, which she put aside after completion, in favor of a more-conventional performance piece. The 'Scarlett Version' was not released until it appeared on the deluxe edition of her 2007 compilation *Crystal Visions*.

The success of 'Stop Draggin' My Heart Around,' made a return appearance by Tom Petty and the Heartbreakers almost inevitable. Petty's composition 'I Will Run To You' offers a similar groove to their earlier song, but the vocals miss the mark of their previous performances together. Still, at the time, Nicks said she enjoyed singing it, and felt 'honored' that Petty wrote it for her, and it's a testament to their already strong relationship that he did so without even being asked. Nicks returned the favor the following year by singing on his demo of 'The Apartment Song,' which he re-recorded in 1989 for his first solo record *Full Moon Fever*.

'Nothing Ever Changes' is the third songwriting collaboration between Stevie Nicks and Sandy Stewart on *The Wild Heart*. Stewart wrote the music, and Nicks crafted the lyric for what she described as 'the only cynical song on this album.' She commented on her songwriting process in the album's press kit: 'When I'm writing, I'll go and drag out 500 pages of lyrics, and take a word here, a line from there, a verse from there ... and it doesn't really matter since I always start from my basic idea and go back to my words.'

If it's me that's driving you to this madness
Then there's one thing that I'd like to say
Take a look at your life and your lovers
Nothing ever changes

Comparing Nicks' comments about 'Sable On Blond' from the time of the album's original release and its 2016 re-release, is remarkable for how certain details can put a story in a completely different light. In 1983, she said, 'I moved into my new dream house, but it was more of a nightmare because it was cold and empty. I only had my piano, there were no phones, and I was all alone, freezing with nothing.' Her 2016 account of the song's origins is similar, but puts it in the context of her relationship with Jimmy Iovine. 'There was a point where I was living in this new house on Sunset in the Palisades. We hadn't broken up, but we weren't living together. The living room was round, surrounded by windows, and in it I had my white Steinway piano and my black Bösendorfer. And I would sit between those two pianos and imagine, 'Jimmy is driving by'.' Those thoughts fed into the lines 'Have you come to see that my face is not seen? ... outside my frost-covered windows?', and musically the song connected to one of her most famous compositions about a relationship ending: 'I wanted to write another song similar to 'Dreams.' Since I only know three chords on the piano, I used my 'Dreams' chords, but sang a completely different melody over it.' Further connecting the song to Fleetwood Mac was the presence of Mick Fleetwood, making him the first member of the band to appear on one of Nicks' solo records.

Fleetwood also played a part in the album closer 'Beauty And The Beast': another song where movie fantasy and personal reality merge. The melancholy lyric aptly evokes literary/visual artist Jean Cocteau's gorgeous film version of the classic fairy tale 'La Belle et la Bête'.

My darling lives in a world that is not mine
An old child misunderstood, out of time
Timeless is the creature who is wise
And timeless is the prisoner in disguise

However, Nicks also had her short-lived romance with Mick Fleetwood in mind. She considered in the 2016 liner notes: 'This handsome 6'5" man was the beast to me, absolutely. Or maybe I was the beast. That's what the song is about: which of us is the beast? There were points where I felt we switched characters.' To capture that mood, Nicks recorded the track accompanied by a full orchestra and fellow singers Sharon Celani and Lori Perry. Nicks first adopted the orchestral approach in the mid-2000s for a recording of 'Landslide,' with uninspiring results, but she deserves credit for giving 'Beauty And The Beast' the full measure of her devotion.

The additional material included on the 2016 deluxe edition of *The Wild Heart* is interesting but not especially revealing. Completists were probably grateful for a CD release of 'Garbo' – another ode to the movies, first released as the B-side of 'Stand Back.' The alternate versions of 'Sable On Blond' and the title song also make for interesting comparisons with those on the album. At the same time, none of them would've felt out of place on the record itself. Similarly, none of the other demos, soundtrack contributions or outtakes suggest *The Wild Heart* is anything other than the album Nicks set out to make. Three are arguably superior to certain songs on the album itself, and Nicks revisited each of them. 'I Sing For The Things' appeared on her next album *Rock A Little*, while the other two resurfaced in the 21st century. 'All The Beautiful Worlds' was re-recorded for the *24 Karat Gold* album, while 'Sorcerer' took a particularly winding road.

Nicks wrote 'Sorcerer' around the time of the *Buckingham Nicks* album, and the duo played it in concert prior to joining Fleetwood Mac. Then singer Marilyn Martin recorded the song for the soundtrack to the 1984 movie *Streets of Fire*, with Jimmy Iovine producing and Nicks singing background vocals along with Sharon Celani and Lori Perry. Nearly two decades later, Nicks produced a new version of the song – with Sheryl Crow as co-producer – for her 2001 record *Trouble In Shangri-La*.

In contrast to the abbreviated tour that followed the release of *Bella Donna*, Nicks toured the United States more extensively to promote *The Wild Heart*, with The Eagles' Joe Walsh as her opening act. After a warm-up show in Las Vegas and performing at Steve Wozniak's second (and final) US Festival in late May, the tour began in earnest on 21 June, shortly after the album's release.

Interviewed by Andrew Means of *Arizona Republic* ahead of a September show in Tempe to benefit City of Hope, Nicks observed that her second solo album represented freedom from Fleetwood Mac. This comment would doubtless have disappointed Mick Fleetwood, whose dedication to the band's survival remained undiminished. By that point, Fleetwood had released a second album of his own, though calling *I'm Not Me* a *solo album* would be a slight misnomer. Credited to Mick Fleetwood's Zoo – a loose musical collective then based around the drummer's California estate (nicknamed The Blue Whale) – the record coalesced when the drummer's initial plans to repeat the approach taken in Brazil on *The Visitor*, dissipated.

I'm Not Me – Mick Fleetwood's Zoo (1983)

Personnel:
Billy Burnette: vocals, guitar
Mick Fleetwood: drums, percussion
George Hawkins: vocals, bass
Steve Ross: guitar, vocals

Additional personnel:
Lindsey Buckingham: guitar, keyboards, vocals
Jon Clarke, Vince Denham: saxophone
Christine McVie: keyboards, vocals
Don Roberts: saxophone
Todd Sharp: lead guitar, rhythm guitar
Ron Thompson: guitar
Producers: Mick Fleetwood, Richard Dashut
Release date: 24 June 1983
Chart places: US: -, UK: -
Running Time: 39:25
Side One: 1. 'Angel Come Home' (Carl Wilson, Geoffrey Cushing-Murray),
2. 'You Might Need Somebody' (Tom Snow, Nan O'Byrne), 3. 'Tonight'
(Annie McLoone),
4. 'I Want You Back' (Buckingham, Steve Ross), 5. 'I'm Not Me' (Billy
Burnette, Michael Smotherman)
Side Two: 1. 'State Of The Art' (George Hawkins), 2. 'Tear It Up' (Johnny
Burnette, Dorsey Burnette, Paul Burlison), 3. 'This Love' (George Hawkins,
Richard Dashut), 4. 'I Give' (Steve Ross), 5. 'Just Because' (Lloyd Price), 6.
'Put Me Right' (George Hawkins)

**Fleetwood discussed the genesis of *I'm Not Me* in an interview included
in the record company press kit:**

It was tentatively planned that I would go down to South America with
George Hawkins: just the two of us. RCA has a studio in Rio, and we
were going to go down there and then bring the stuff back that we'd
recorded with other people there, and do whatever we needed to do in
a studio here, just as we did with *The Visitor*. But then Fleetwood Mac
toured, and I realized I wasn't going to be able to hack a trip to South
America, so we bought a (recording) board and other equipment, and
ended up making most of the album at my house in Malibu. The basic
band was George, myself and Steve Ross. I was becoming really good
friends with Billy (Burnette), and he started hanging out a bit, then he
just became part of the entity and part of the album.

**Billy Burnette, who played guitar and sang in the Zoo, personified the
mix of contemporary and classic on *I'm Not Me*. The guitarist's father
Dorsey Burnette and uncle Johnny Burnette were both part of the**

influential rockabilly group The Rock and Roll Trio. After that group disbanded in 1957, the pair wrote songs that became hits for Ricky Nelson: including 'It's Late,' which reached the top 10 in the US and UK. Despite none of the Rock and Roll Trio's singles charting in the US, they developed a cult following, and The Beatles and The Yardbirds played their songs. That legacy continued when Billy – who took up the family business before he was even a teenager – performed The Rock and Roll Trio classic 'Tear It Up' with Fleetwood and company.

I'm Not Me as a whole was a mix of covers and originals, spanning the recent Beach Boys song 'Angel Come Home' and the Lindsey Buckingham co-write 'I Want You Back.' Buckingham sang and played throughout the album, as did Christine McVie. While Mick Fleetwood wanted the Zoo to feel like a band in its own right, their presence – along with Richard Dashut co-producing – gave *I'm Not Me* the strongest ties to Fleetwood Mac of any of the band members' outside albums in this period.

As one interviewer noted at the time, the album echoed the Fleetwood Mac pattern by having three different lead vocalists. Unfortunately, even with the connections to Fleetwood's better-known band and a catchy new Buckingham co-write (complete with the now-obligatory music video), the album sold poorly. It didn't chart in either the US or the UK, and, like *The Visitor*, had very limited CD availability. Lack of critical attention didn't help the record either, though retrospective reviews have been favorable – such as The *All Music Guide* calling it 'an overlooked little gem of early-'80s mainstream pop/rock.'

The *All Music Guide*'s broader assessment of *I'm Not Me* applies perfectly to its opening track. While The Beach Boys had remained popular in spite of personal, professional and creative struggles, the period of their work that other artists were likely to record was over a decade in the past, but the Zoo covered 'Angel Come Home': a track from their 1979 record *L.A. (Light Album)*. But Mick Fleetwood had a different sort of relationship with The Beach Boys – and their periodically estranged drummer Dennis Wilson – than most. Fleetwood said: 'I was familiar with 'Angel Come Home' before it turned up on an album. I used to play it with Dennis hanging out in a garage, you know. I always thought it was a lovely song, a sweet song, real emotive. One night at home, Billy was there, and amongst a huge mound of disorganized cassettes, I found – it was sort of like radar – a cassette of that song.' The end result was a cover that outdoes the original. Though heartfelt, the Beach Boys' rendition seems stuck in a no-man's-land between their classic 1960s style and the following decade's efforts to evolve musically as circumstances lessened Brian Wilson's involvement. In the Zoo's version, the harmonies evoke the Beach Boys sound, while Billy Burnette's lead vocal offers a mix of vulnerability and swagger also in keeping with the older band's spirit.

The solo albums by Fleetwood Mac's singer-songwriters made their contributions to the group's work apparent through what they wrote and – especially in Buckingham's case – how they recorded them. Mick Fleetwood's influence is felt not just in his playing, but also his critical role in the choice of which material his bands recorded: 'I suppose my role is to nurture a situation. People started bringing in songs, like George (Hawkins) and Steve (Ross). Steve's a really talented young man, and, coincidentally, he made a couple of albums with The Beach Boys. He started writing little bits, and Richard (Dashut) and I kept saying, 'C'mon, finish the song!'

While this process tilted the balance toward originals written within the group, the covers are still worthy. Along with 'Angel Come Home,' Lloyd Price's 'Just Because' and the family affair of 'Tear It Up' evoking an earlier era of rock, 'You Might Need Somebody' and 'Tonight' represented then-current songwriting talent. 'You Might Need Somebody' – which had been a UK hit for American R&B singer Randy Crawford, was co-written by Tom Snow, whose work has been recorded by Bonnie Raitt, Christina Aguilera and Dolly Parton, among many others. Parton also recorded a song by the writer of 'Tonight': Annie McLoone. An artist in her own right, McLoone had been in Fleetwood Mac's orbit since the late-1970s when she sang backing vocals with Stevie Nicks on Walter Egan's 'Magnet And Steel', a recording that also featured her partner – and former Buckingham Nicks bassist – Tom Moncrieff. She and Moncrieff also helped Nicks with the demo of 'Sara' during the *Tusk* sessions, and their personal and professional relationships continued into the 21st century.

Of the original songs on the album, Buckingham's input ensured that 'I Want You Back' sounded the most like Fleetwood Mac. The track was released as a single, complete with a cinema-inspired music video featuring Fleetwood as Ivan The Terrible. But despite getting some airplay, it missed the charts.

Buckingham's own single 'Holiday Road' – one of two songs director Harold Ramis asked him to write for the movie *National Lampoon's*

Vacation – fared somewhat better. Between cover versions and the guitarist's live performances, the song's cultural life far outstrips the expectations one might have for a song that only reached 82 on the US Hot 100 and didn't chart at all in the UK.

While the album's title song and 'State Of The Art' lean more towards straightforward rock and roll, and 'This Love' is a nifty pop song, the more-mellow songs 'I Give' and 'Put Me Right' are more-remarkable for what they show about Mick Fleetwood. In a remarkable demonstration of ego sublimation, he doesn't play drums on either, and only percussion on the latter. Based on Fleetwood's comments at the time, this stemmed from a genuine desire to make the Zoo an entity in its own right: 'I wanted some onward-going community spirit so people would feel part of a growing entity. How far it goes and what it grows into, who knows? No, it's not Fleetwood Mac, and it hasn't got the years and emotion behind it. But all these people are very close, and they enjoy working together.'

As with *Fleetwood Mac* and *Tusk*, Mick certainly put in the effort to promote *I'm Not Me*. The drummer displayed his characteristic wry humour when writing about the tour in his 1990 autobiography:

> Lord knows we tried to make the Zoo album a hit, touring throughout America. We bought ourselves tuxedos, and played bars – traveling by bus, the old-fashioned way. It was like a scene from Spinal Tap: we'd arrive at these clubs and there be nobody there. The lads in the band were embarrassed for me when we'd go out and play for 50 people. But I loved it. It was a total failure, and a lot of fun.

The group nevertheless played a few high-profile shows. Their November concert at the Bottom Line in New York was favorably reviewed in the *New York Times*, and their appearance on *Saturday Night Live* gave the Zoo a bigger audience than any other show on the tour – even the one on Maui where Stevie Nicks joined them onstage and attracted a crowd of thousands. Nicks appeared on *Saturday Night Live* the following month, performing 'Stand Back' and 'Nightbird.' Along with Fleetwood Mac's performance of 'Oh Diane' recorded for the 3 February edition of the BBC's long-running TV show *Top Of The Pops*, that appearance bookended 1983 with a *de facto* statement about the state of the band. Though the year began with a rare pop-star moment for Lindsey Buckingham, it closed with a public reminder that Stevie Nicks was the group's brightest star.

1984: Two Kinds of Trouble

Even by the measure of his bandmates, Mick Fleetwood embodied rock star excess. However, when he declared bankruptcy in March 1984, the causes were as appropriate for the business section of the newspaper as its entertainment page. Fleetwood's legendary drug habit played its part, as did his love of cars. But what really hurt him financially was punishing interest rates on real estate loans – such as the reported 17 per cent rate on the $1,600,000 mortgage on The Blue Whale. Combined with a steep decline in his income as Fleetwood Mac became less active and his own musical ventures failed to catch on, the fiscal crunch led to The Blue Whale and his other belongings being sold off to pay his many creditors.

After Sara Recor left him to rejoin 'the real world,' Fleetwood moved in with Richard Dashut and focused on getting his life back into something resembling order. In the short term, this meant playing poorly-attended shows with the Zoo – even after RCA dropped his contract – while hoping Fleetwood Mac would reunite. On a more fundamental level, Fleetwood recalled a sense of relief 'that my father hadn't lived to see the day.'

Christine McVie (1984)
Personnel:
Christine McVie: vocals, keyboards, percussion
Todd Sharp: guitar, vocals
George Hawkins: bass, vocals
Steve Ferrone: drums, percussion
Additional personnel:
Lindsey Buckingham: guitar ('Got A Hold on Me', 'So Excited', 'The Smile I Live For'; backing vocals ('The Challenge', 'Who's Dreaming This Dream', 'The Smile I Live For'
Eric Clapton: lead guitar ('The Challenge')
Ray Cooper: percussion ('The Challenge', 'So Excited', 'Ask Anybody', 'The Smile I Live For'
Mick Fleetwood: drums ('Ask Anybody')
Eddy Quintela: additional keyboards ('The Smile I Live For')
Steve Winwood: lead and backing vocals ('One In A Million'); keyboards, backing vocals ('Ask Anybody'); synthesizer ('Got A Hold On Me', 'One In A Million', 'The Smile I Live For'
Producer: Russ Titleman
Engineer: David Richards

Release date: 27 January 1984
Chart places: US: 26, UK: 58
Running Time: 43:48
Side One: 1. 'Love Will Show Us How' (McVie, Todd Sharp), 2. 'The Challenge' (McVie, Sharp), 3. 'So Excited' (McVie, Sharp, Billy Burnette), 4. 'One In A Million' (McVie, Sharp), 5. 'Ask Anybody' (McVie, Steve Winwood)
Side Two: 1. 'Got A Hold On Me' (McVie, Sharp), 2. 'Who's Dreaming This Dream' (Sharp, Daniel Douma), 3. 'I'm The One' (Sharp), 4. 'Keeping Secrets' (Sharp, Alan Pasqua), 5. 'The Smile I Live For' (McVie)

At the other end of the telescope, a June 1984 *Rolling Stone* profile presented Christine McVie as 'the epitome of rock & roll sanity.' As in his review of *The Wild Heart* the year before, writer Christopher Connelly overstated things here. Still, the description fit a broader perception of McVie (who was referred to with the expression 'Earth mother' in multiple previous articles) – one that was inevitably relative to others in her sphere: Stevie Nicks among them. Reflecting the emerging distance between band members at the time, McVie said, 'She seems to have developed her own fantasy world somehow, which I'm not a part of. We don't socialize much.'

While Christine McVie's personal life lacked the overt drama surrounding Nicks or some other stars, neither was it untouched by tragedy. On 4 January 1984, her troubled former boyfriend Dennis Wilson was buried at sea off the coast of California. In the years since their relationship ended, Wilson had gotten married again and had another son, but his self-destructive tendencies remained consistent. Nevertheless, McVie was stunned upon learning that Wilson had drowned on 28 December 1983 while swimming near his boat in the Pacific Ocean. McVie recalled in *Rolling Stone*: 'My secretary called me up at eight in the morning. I knew something. She said, 'Dennis drowned today,' and my first reaction was to say, 'My god, is he alright?' I still really can't believe it. He just seemed indestructible.'

In later years, McVie's initial shock was complemented by another sort of disbelief. She told Robin Eggar in a 2004 interview for a supplement for the Sunday Express: 'I was surprised he survived as long as he did, to be honest. He was asking for it all his life.' McVie opted for more stability in her life during the 1980s. She met keyboardist Eddy Quintela while recording her self-titled solo album in late 1983, and they soon settled into a long-term relationship before marrying in 1986. Beyond the domestic, Quintela also wrote numerous songs with McVie for the Fleetwood Mac albums that followed.

Despite being this incarnation of Fleetwood Mac's most accomplished writer of pop songs, McVie was the last of the three to turn her attention to a solo album after the band agreed to see other people in the wake of *Tusk*. While promoting *Christine McVie* – released in January 1984 – she admitted to having had mixed feelings about stepping outside the group setting, hinting that she only took the step because, 'It had reached a point where this record was expected of me.' Much of the album was recorded at two storied sites – Mountain Studios in Montreux, Switzerland (which at the time was owned by Queen), and London's Olympic Studios. But a more-intimate location also played a part. Steve Winwood had already achieved success with the Spencer Davis Group, and left to form Traffic when McVie joined Fleetwood Mac. After Traffic disbanded, Winwood turned part of his house in Gloucestershire into a studio so he could work on music at his own pace – including *Arc of a Diver*: the successful album that established him as a solo artist. Winwood was just a couple of years away from the fully-fledged stardom his next album – 1986's *Back in the High Life* – would bring him, but in 1983 he was just helping out a fellow musician.

Other musicians on the record included Eric Clapton, longtime Elton John percussionist Ray Cooper, and Average White Band drummer Steve Ferrone who was recommended by producer Russ Titelman. Along with guest appearances from Lindsey Buckingham and Mick Fleetwood, they helped make *Christine McVie* second only to *Bella Donna* for Fleetwood Mac solo albums featuring high-profile musicians. Their presence, along with George Hawkins and Todd Sharp who formed the album's core band along with Steve Ferrone, added to the Fleetwood Mac connection, both musicians having played on *The Visitor* and *I'm Not Me*.

Because the songs themselves – even those McVie wasn't involved in writing – leaned into her trademark style, and the majority featured her bandmates in some fashion, the album bore the closest resemblance to Fleetwood Mac of any of their 1980s solo albums. However, this similarity was a mixed blessing. The stylistic consistency that fostered the two top-30 US singles 'Got A Hold On Me' and 'Love Will Show Us How' – either of which could've been highlights on a Fleetwood Mac album – also meant that some compositions felt quite ordinary. This was reflected in the reviews, where critics found the qualities that were benefits in the group setting, to be less appealing on a solo basis. *People* magazine's review praised the album's songwriting and 'loose, good-time feeling,' but found McVie's singing to be underwhelming, judging her duet with Steve Winwood on 'One In A Million' to be the rare case where she wasn't overshadowed by collaborators. Conversely, Stephen Holden's review in the *New York Times* saw that song as a failed attempt to mirror the dynamic Stevie Nicks developed with Tom Petty, dismissing both Christine's singing and the songs as, on the whole, bland. In retrospect, it seems likely that critics had picked up on McVie's initial reticence about doing a solo album at all. In any case, after the muted reception in the US and UK, McVie was apparently content to remain – as *Rolling Stone*'s two-star review put it – 'the strong, silent center of Fleetwood Mac.' Though she did a brief tour – memorialized with a concert-video release – the singer didn't release another solo album until 2004.

Though not entirely successful in this effort, Christine McVie's decision to write most her solo album's songs with other musicians, stemmed from a desire to diversify its sound: 'I felt a whole record of just my music might become tiresome. I think the record has so much more variety than it probably would have if I had written all the songs on my own.' Whatever its shortcomings, 'Love Will Show Us How' starts the album strongly, and was one of eight songs she co-wrote with Todd Sharp: a partnership that emerged as a happy accident. 'I knew Todd Sharp was the guitar player I wanted, but I wasn't aware when I made that decision that I might do as much writing with him as I actually did.'

Whatever her ambivalence about working as a solo act, McVie still indulged in the expected accompaniments to the music business. In 1984, this meant music videos. The worst that can be said of the lighthearted clip for 'Love Will Show Us How,' is that its send-up of performance videos – in which everyone that could go wrong, *does* – isn't as much fun as the track it's promoting. A companion piece to the *Mirage* track 'Love in Store,' the song acknowledges that even strong relationships are not immune from doubt, but it never loses its fundamental optimism.

I don't know how
Love will survive
But it's all right for now
Still I believe
Love will show us how

While the album rarely exceeds expectations, neither do its shortcomings sink to a level fans would find disastrous. 'The Challenge' is a case in point – a noticeable step-down in quality from the opening track, but still possessing virtues. The song has a pleasing melody, complemented but not overshadowed by Eric Clapton's guitar work. The only downside lies in the sentiments, which seem drawn from a self-help book rather than experience.

On every corner you turn
There's a heartache
Well, love's a challenge
A chance that you've gotta take

'So Excited' is more lively. Zoo member Billy Burnette brings a more-traditional rock-and-roll sensibility to the McVie/Sharp songwriting tandem. In keeping with the throwback feel, the lyric is slight but fits the sonic setting well.

Well, I know any minute
He'll be knocking on my front door
I just can't wait
I can't wait a minute more

Side one of *Christine McVie* concludes with her two Steve Winwood collaborations. Though it comes after 'One In A Million' on the album, 'Ask Anybody' was the first song they worked on – the culmination of what McVie recalled as two decades of admiration for Winwood:

I met Steve briefly during the old Spencer Davis Group days about 20 years ago, and he's always been my idol. Since I was doing a solo record, I thought I would try to get in touch with him to see if he fancied doing a song with me. I flew to England, and I stayed at his house in Gloucester, where he has a beautiful brand-new studio in a converted barn. At first we were both very edgy and nervous about working together, so we went down to the pub and socked back a few pints, and then we went to his studio. The song really came easily. We just got about six different ideas together, and chose the best one.

Though Winwood wrote 'Ask Anybody' with McVie, he only sang on the chorus. His presence is more audible on 'One In A Million,' which anticipated the soul inflections Winwood was later to pursue on *Back in the High Life*. McVie said, 'Steve heard 'One In A Million' and said he wanted to sing on it. So I suggested he take the second verse, and we did that song as a duet.'

If he tells you he needs you
Don't turn around
He's one in a million
Don't turn him down

Winwood also played keyboards on what was side two's opening track and McVie's sole top-10 US hit as a solo artist: 'Got A Hold On Me'. Thanks to the chorus harmonies and Lindsey Buckingham on guitar, it sounds the most like a Fleetwood Mac song of anything on the album, even without Mick playing drums. This applies to the lyric as well, which McVie delivers in her quintessentially-lovelorn fashion.

Well, I've been in love and I've lost
I can count the tears
But I can't count the cost

'Who's Dreaming This Dream' is the first of three consecutive songs that McVie wasn't involved in writing, and one that gets a better performance from her than the song probably deserves. The next track, 'I'm the One' written solely by Todd Sharp, is much better. Sharp's guitar playing echoes his name, and McVie's vocal matches it.

But you don't understand the heartache behind my kiss
You're just thankful for a friend
I'm not your doctor baby
I'm not your psychiatrist
But you keep comin' back again

Of all the songs on *Christine McVie*, 'Keeping Secrets' does the most to justify the lukewarm reviews that greeted the album. As a composition and a performance, it isn't bad so much as unexciting. Fortunately, 'The Smile I Live For' is more-dynamic. The album's only song that McVie wrote alone, it concludes the record with the same sense of drama-writ-small that typifies her best work.

You were the lonely one
Thought I had you on the run
But now I guess it's me
Begging you, begging you

Like 'Got A Hold On Me,' 'The Smile I Live For' benefits from perfectly-judged musical support from Steve Winwood and Lindsey Buckingham. According to McVie, 'Lindsey came over to Montreux for a week. He was in London looking for an engineer to finish his album, so I asked him to nip over since he was so close by.'

Go Insane – Lindsey Buckingham (1984)

Personnel:
Lindsey Buckingham: vocals, guitar, keyboards, bass, percussion, Fairlight CMI, LinnDrum, pump organ, lap harp
Additional personnel:
Gordon Fordyce: keyboards, cowbell ('I Want You'); howling ('Play In The Rain')
Bryant Simpson: bass ('Go Insane')
Producers: Lindsey Buckingham, Gordon Fordyce
Executive producer: Roy Thomas Baker
Assistant engineer: John Boghosian
Release date: 30 July 1984
Chart places: US: 45, UK: -
Running Time: 38:20
All songs written by Lindsey Buckingham, except where noted.
Side One: 1. 'I Want You' (Buckingham, Fordyce), 2. 'Go Insane', 3. 'Slow Dancing', 4. 'I Must Go', 5. 'Play In The Rain'
Side Two: 1. 'Play In The Rain (Continued)', 2. 'Loving Cup', 3. 'Bang The Drum', 4. 'D.W. Suite'

Buckingham's second solo album *Go Insane* was released that summer, and reflected major personal and creative developments for the guitarist. After several years together, he and girlfriend Carol Ann Harris, split up in 1983. The two had met while Harris was a receptionist at Producer's Workshop, the Los Angeles studio where Fleetwood Mac was putting finishing touches on *Rumours*, and she soon became Buckingham's first serious girlfriend since the breakup with Stevie Nicks.

Like so many aspects of Fleetwood Mac's history, the narrative diverges based on who's telling the story and when. Lindsey and Carol's relationship features prominently in a 1984 *Rolling Stone* article about Buckingham, which includes commentary from the former couple, Buckingham's brother Jeff, and Richard Dashut. One of the guitarist's closest friends during this period, Dashut's comments hint at an intense relationship, echoed by Harris' observation: 'I don't think I can remember relaxing the whole time I was with him.' However, the producer also described the couple as 'very much in love,' and the early years of the relationship as 'one of the happiest times in (Buckingham's) life.' Over time, the couple's happiness apparently gave way to the familiar refrain of substance abuse, with Jeff Buckingham recalling a 'sweet young girl' who 'changed into a music-hardened, drug-hardened person.' Harris admitted to over-indulging in cocaine at the time, adding that Lindsey also had a problem with the drug: a claim the guitarist denied.

Two decades later, in her 2007 memoir *Storms*, Harris went into much greater detail about her relationship with Buckingham, alleging numerous incidents of emotional and physical abuse on his part, and all-around debauchery in Fleetwood Mac's orbit. Buckingham, who was married with children when *Storms* was published, doesn't comment on her allegations, and has said very little about the problems in their relationship in the 1980s: at least in print. Though he admitted to personal problems between them and that their relationship existed in 'a world of people who were not particularly responsible,' he declined to go into detail. He told the Rolling Stone interviewer: 'I don't really want to talk about that. I don't think it would be very fair. I think it would hurt her.' This view was apparently limited to spoken remarks because Buckingham acknowledged that the breakup fed into the songs on *Go Insane*. The album was dedicated to Harris, who had mixed emotions about that, finding the record hard to listen to, while also telling *Rolling Stone*, 'I think there's a lot of love there.' Buckingham defended the choice of subject as a matter of mental health in both *Rolling Stone* and a profile in *Musician* the same year. He told the latter publication: 'Getting this stuff down on vinyl was a lot better than going to see a shrink.' Though less colorful, other comments from the *Musician* article point to Carol Ann Harris not being the only relationship weighing on him. 'The whole experience of Fleetwood Mac has been a sense of responding to other people's needs: sometimes ahead of my own.'

Having to make peace with Fleetwood Mac's more-conservative post-*Tusk* musical approach is a recurring theme in articles about Lindsey Buckingham's work. Discussing his music in a 2021 piece on the website

Uproxx, he talked about *Go Insane* as a major step in that process, contrasting the 'grounded place' he found himself in there artistically with the 'more-ironic' approach expressed on *Law and Order*. In Elektra Records' album press kit, he observed that 'The lyrical and musical thread running from song to song is stronger this time, and there's more of a singular feeling about the album as a whole.'

Another contrast with the previous record was in the use of technology. Where *Law and Order* – and, to some extent, *Mirage* – displayed a more-retro approach, *Go Insane* was assertively up to date, especially in its use of the Fairlight CMI – a computer/keyboard hybrid also used by Peter Gabriel and Stevie Wonder. Buckingham said, 'You had a million different sounds, from drums to horns to strings to voices. It wasn't synthesized. It was all sampled. For someone who defined their creative process through this painting process – at least for solo work – that was a natural progression.'

In British magazine *Kerrang!*, Buckingham said, 'I hope people will perceive me as someone attempting to push back the barriers of pop music.' While *Go Insane*'s title track was a hit in the US, the album's disappointing sales invite the question of whether he failed or actually succeeded beyond his aspirations, but just a bit too soon. As usual for the guitarist, critics were more-impressed, both in music-focused publications such as Kerrang!, and more-mainstream outlets like *People* magazine.

After finding the recent albums by Christine McVie and Stevie Nicks disappointing, *Rolling Stone* writer Christopher Connelly finally found a Fleetwood Mac-related project to be enthusiastic about. Despite finding some of its sonic digressions repetitive, he discussed the album as a potential artistic breakthrough for rock music in general, 'representing as it does the most successful combination yet of hummable '70s slick rock and '80s avant-edge.' Connelly concluded the review by comparing *Go Insane* to The Beach Boys' landmark album *Pet Sounds*. As much as Buckingham admired Brian Wilson and viewed him as a kindred spirit, Buckingham probably would've demurred that particular album comparison. In any case, he thought enough of the album to include five of its eight tracks and a live rendition of the title song on his 2018 compilation *Solo Anthology: The Best of Lindsey Buckingham*.

I want you
I guess I had to prove
I want you
I was someone hard to lose

Following the spoken introduction to 'I Want You' – which culminates in the above admission – side one of *Go Insane* offers a string of four well-crafted but decidedly off-kilter pop songs. For an artist who doesn't consider himself as a songwriter in the traditional sense, Lindsey Buckingham is quite adept at the form. 'I Want You' balances a straightforward hook with more expansive textures instrumentally and vocally. Recognizing that his painterly approach had the potential downside of making it 'hard to judge when something has reached its most satisfying conclusion,' Buckingham worked with Gordon Fordyce as his co-producer and Roy Thomas Baker as executive producer. Over the course of a decade, Baker had produced bestselling albums by The Cars and Queen, while Fordyce was a relative newcomer who'd previously worked as an engineer on albums by The Boomtown Rats, Mötley Crüe and Hazel O'Connor. Nevertheless, Buckingham determined Fordyce to be a better choice for this particular album than regular collaborator Richard Dashut. Buckingham told *Kerrang!*: 'Whilst I did consider involving him once more, I believe that he's become too much like me, and thus offers no counterpoint. Gordon brought a freshness and a new sparkle into the studio.' That contribution went beyond the technical, with Fordyce co-writing and playing keyboards on 'I Want You' – one of only two songs on the album where someone other than Buckingham played an instrumental part.

The title track is the other. MTV airplay for the song's surreal video, filled with shifting perspectives and flourishes (including a guitar playing itself), probably made 'Go Insane' feel like a bigger hit than its peak at 23 on the *Billboard* Hot 100 would suggest. Even putting aside any specific inspiration from Buckingham's personal relationships, the song conveys the weight of having lived in a tabloid-friendly environment.

> Two kinds of trouble in this world
> Livin', dying
> I lost my power in this world
> And the rumours are flying

Concert performances of 'Go Insane' are a further testament to its power. Whether on his own or with Fleetwood Mac, Buckingham strips away the impeccable production in favor of a stark solo rendition with just vocals and guitar – another striking gesture for someone who doesn't see songwriting as their strength.

There was also a music video for the next track, 'Slow Dancing'. Filled with dancing ghosts and Buckingham looking aristocratic in a haunted house, it was similarly eye-catching but little-seen. While it missed the charts when released as the album's second single, 'Slow Dancing' is the best pop composition on *Go Insane*, fusing classic lyric elements, thoroughly modern production and a healthy dose of desire.

> The nighttime filled with a cold winter chill
> The rain is music on my window sill
> I come up fast, I go down slow
> So tell me darlin', do you want to go
> (Let's go) Slow dancing in the moonlight
> (Let's go) Want to slow dance with you all night

In 2018, Buckingham told the website *Stereogum*: "Slow Dancing' was kind of a contemplation on the romantic notion that often happens when you're young and you're in a situation where there's seemingly a range of possibilities at any given time. And if you're out of a relationship ... It's funny how whenever I would connect with someone, you always try to give it a level of at least romantic aspiration, if nothing else, because you want to make a human connection.' The fractured connection with Carol Ann Harris comes through on 'I Must Go' – the song on *Go Insane* that seems most directly inspired by her. The melodic momentum is counterbalanced by lyric interjections of 'Hey little girl, leave the little drug alone' alternating with 'Hey little girl, you're leaving me all alone.' The end result conveys concern that was genuine but perhaps not entirely selfless on the singer's part.

After four relatively straightforward songs, 'Play In The Rain' is a striking departure. Featuring a minimal lyric revolving around the phrase 'Can we play in the rain,' it bridges the album's two sides. However, because Buckingham doesn't develop the piece musically until the very end, the combined two parts of more than seven minutes become repetitive, making an abrupt rather than considered transition from side one's overtly pop-oriented pieces. The album might've been better served by going straight into 'Loving Cup.'

Despite being one of the longer songs on *Go Insane*, it never loses focus. Set to a Bo Diddley beat, the guitars and electronics interplay is used in service of a much stronger lyric and vocal approach than 'Play In The Rain'.

Resurrection of original sin
Calls to me on the midnight wind
You are the object of my desire
Open your mouth
Put out the fire

Mixing hypnotic synthesizer patterns and keening vocals, the penultimate track 'Bang The Drum' presents a fusion of new wave and *Pet Sounds*-style pop. Like the Beach Boys record, the song has an affecting heart-on-its-sleeve quality.

Afraid to move
Afraid to lose
A piece of faith
A piece of heart

'Bang The Drum' precedes a track with an even-more-pronounced Beach Boys influence. Described by Buckingham as 'musical cinema,' the three-part 'D.W. Suite' offered an earnest tribute to Dennis Wilson. In the first section, 'The Wish,' lines such as 'If we go, go insane/We can all go together', which fit Wilson's reckless image, mesh with a melody evoking the 19th-century folk song 'Wild Mountain Thyme'.

The musical wake continues in the second segment, 'The Prayer,' in which the arrangement and sentiments expressed ('Pray for guidance from above/Shadow all your hopes with love') telegraphed that Dennis wasn't the only Wilson family member Buckingham had in mind. He explained the thoughts behind the song in *Kerrang!*:

I also did it as a way of tipping my hat to Brian Wilson, who was the driving force behind the band. I've always identified with Brian, because he has spent years attempting to take what was essentially a successful early-'60s pop band in a more adventurous and challenged direction. Yet the pressure put upon him by the other members of the BBs and even his own family because of the desire to experiment and change, has been incredible.

Buckingham's place within Fleetwood Mac was a recurring theme in the articles about *Go Insane*. While uncertainty about the band's future was a constant, the guitarist's feelings on that point, varied considerably from one article to the next. He told *Rock* magazine: 'We certainly haven't broken up, and we will do another studio album at some point.'

However, his *Kerrang!* comments were far more pessimistic: 'If you're asking me should Fleetwood Mac continue, at this point in time, my answer must be... *NO!* I don't see any reason to carry on with the band just because certain people have hit financial troubles.' The desire to carve out an identity distinct from Fleetwood Mac, showed through in the same article in comments about plans to tour on his own: 'I'd like to tour as soon as I possibly can under my own name, but I want to wait until another Lindsey Buckingham album has been put out so that any show can contain only solo material. I don't want to be in the position of having to throw in classic Fleetwood Mac tunes to fill in the gaps.'

Buckingham started working on his next solo album soon after *Go Insane*, but events took a very different path, and his first solo tour had to wait until 1992. In the interim, his lone live appearance would be at Get Tough On Toxics – an August 1986 benefit concert supporting environmental initiatives in California. The show's lineup included Stevie Nicks and Don Henley – complete with the obligatory duet on 'Leather And Lace.' And despite Buckingham's desire to emphasize his solo work, his brief performance featured two Fleetwood Mac songs.

Left: Christine McVie was reluctant to record a solo album and only relented because she felt one was expected of her. (*Warner Bros.*)

Right: The 1984 single 'Go Insane' from the album of the same name, became Lindsey Buckingham's second - and final - Top 40 hit in the US. (*Reprise*)

Left: Recorded with a variety of producers, Stevie Nicks' 1985 album *Rock a Little* was inconsistent but still popular. (*Modern*)

1985: Put The Blame On Me If You Want To

As the only true constant for the entirety of their career, no one
displayed a deeper commitment to Fleetwood Mac than Mick Fleetwood:
which made the early-to-mid-1980s a trying time for him. He was
disappointed that the band didn't tour more for *Mirage* in 1982, and
if anything, his financial problems amplified his desire for a reunion.
However, not unlike the management shake-up after the *Tusk* tour,
he was firmly in the minority within the group: a state of affairs
summarized in his 2014 autobiography.

> I continued to play gigs with the Zoo, but all I cared about was getting
> Fleetwood Mac together again. The problem was that I was the only
> one eager to do so at the time. Stevie was enjoying a huge solo career,
> and her second solo album *The Wild Heart*, had sold into the millions.
> Lindsey was working on his third solo release, and Christine had scored
> a hit with 'Got A Hold On Me.' Meanwhile, John was relishing his
> semi-retirement, sailing his boat wherever he pleased and playing the
> occasional gig with John Mayall and The Bluesbreakers.

By the end of 1985, a Fleetwood Mac reunion was underway, but
the path forward turned out to be long and circuitous, even by their
standards. At the beginning of the year, though, the individual efforts
involved one of their members performing on one of the most famous
records of the 1980s. The most surprising thing, is not just which member
but also how little the end product sounded like Fleetwood Mac. For all
his talent and success, Lindsey Buckingham was still a footnote in the
making of the chart-topping USA For Africa single 'We Are the World.'
With a few decades of hindsight, the patchy quality of 'We Are the World'
confirms its legacy as being less about the song than who showed up
for a good cause on 28 January 1985, and the stories surrounding that
recording session. In Buckingham's case, it meant a memorable anecdote
about one of the recording's architects – Michael Jackson – which
Buckingham related to journalist Tim Roxborogh in 2009:

> I think I walked into the bathroom, and he was in there, and it kind of
> freaked him out! He was quite nervous just to be startled by someone
> walking in, and I just nodded my head. I didn't feel comfortable trying
> to engage him in a 'Hello' at that point. He was really at the top of his

game, and I think probably even then was dealing with a lot of demons that were probably from way back when he was a kid. You know, I just didn't want to intrude at all on his trip.

When 'We Are The World' was sung as the finale for the US portion of the Live Aid concert on 13 July 1985, neither Buckingham nor any other Fleetwood Mac member was part of the performance. While the band collectively – or Nicks individually – would've fit Live Aid's aim of offering a global jukebox, they apparently weren't asked. The band's only musical presence that day was in Judas Priest's rendition of Peter Green's 'The Green Manalishi (With the Two Prong Crown)', which had been a mainstay of their live repertoire since the late-1970s.

However, Stevie Nicks *did* perform at a number of smaller-scale benefit shows in 1985. On 17 September, she performed on her own and alongside Tom Petty and the Heartbreakers and Don Henley at a concert supporting Mulholland Tomorrow – an organization working to prevent overdevelopment in the Santa Monica Mountains. Henley – the concert headliner – reprised his duet with Nicks on 'Leather And Lace' two nights later in Tucson, Arizona. That show – with a lineup including Jackson Browne and Stevie Ray Vaughn – was in support of the so-called Sanctuary Movement of churches working to help Central American refugees that ran afoul of US immigration laws.

These benefit performances preceded the release of Nicks' third solo album *Rock a Little* on 18 November. She'd started working on the album that became *Rock a Little* (originally titled *Mirror Mirror,* according to some) soon after *The Wild Heart*, with the intention of releasing it by the end of 1984. But after recording several tracks with Jimmy Iovine, Nicks' professional relationship with the producer followed the path of her personal one, with drug use once again a factor. She told Chris Neal in her 2007 interview for *Performing Songwriter*:

> By the time we got to *Rock a Little*, (Iovine) had *had* it. I didn't blame him. I understood. On *Rock a Little*, we were really slipping into the darkness ... There are some really good things on *Rock a Little*. There are also parts where I go, 'What were you thinking? Did you really think that was good?'

Sometimes artists are their own worst critics, but her retrospective assessment is largely on target. Where *Bella Donna* and *The Wild Heart* conveyed Nicks' stated need to record more of her own songs than she could within Fleetwood Mac, much of *Rock a Little* felt like an exercise in perpetuating her solo career solely for its own sake. The inconsistent combination of tracks produced by Iovine and those made with others producing presented Nicks as an artist with an identity crisis.

Throughout the record, she sounds uncertain whether to submerge her identity in the synth-heavy pop landscape of the mid-1980s or bend it to her will. It's telling that more songs featured a credit for programming electronic instruments than featured guitarist Waddy Wachtel, who'd played such a major role on her previous albums. Many veteran artists indulged in ill-fitting production styles during the 1980s. Some fared better than others, with the quality of the songwriting typically being the deciding factor: an area where *Rock A Little* also struggled.

Both aspects factored into the mixed reviews the album received. *San Francisco Chronicle* reviewer Joel Selvin used the terms 'labored' and 'heavy-handed' to describe its sound, and was unimpressed with Nicks' 'turgid writing.' The *New York Times*' Stephen Holden was similarly critical of her songwriting, but kinder to the production, which he viewed as, 'transforming Miss Nicks' gauzy diaristic musings into sonic dreamscapes.'

For at least a segment of her audience, that was sufficient. *Rock a Little* was certified platinum in the United States, and gold in the UK. While a solo hit single remained elusive in the UK, 'Talk To Me' and 'I Can't Wait' charted at 4 and 16, respectively in the US. Even as the album demonstrated that Nicks was in a better artistic position within Fleetwood Mac, its commercial success ensured that she could maintain her distance from them. That might not have encouraged optimism among fans who preferred her earlier work, but their faith would be rewarded after a fashion.

Rock A Little – Stevie Nicks (1985)

Personnel:
Side One:
1. 'I Can't Wait' (Nicks, Rick Nowels, Eric Pressly)
Stevie Nicks: lead vocals, Sharon Celani, Lori Perry, Marilyn Martin, Maria Vidal: background vocals, Rick Nowels: synthesizer, background vocals, George Black: Dr. 'T' bass, guitar, LinnDrum programming, background vocals, Jamie Sherrif: synthesizer, programming
Mike Landau: guitar
Producers: Rick Nowels, Jimmy Iovine, Engineers: John Kovarek, David

Hernandez

2. 'Rock A Little (Go Ahead Lily)' (Nicks)

Stevie Nicks: lead vocals, Sharon Celani, Lori Perry, Marilyn Martin: background vocals

Kenny Edwards: bass, Waddy Wachtel: guitar, Billy Payne: synthesizer, Steve Jordan: drums

Rick Nowels: synthesizer, Jamie Sherrif: programming, synth strings

Producer: Jimmy Iovine, Engineers: Shelly Yakus, Gabe Veltri

3. 'Sister Honey' (Nicks, Les Dudek)

Stevie Nicks: lead vocals, Sharon Celani, Lori Perry, Marilyn Martin: background vocals, Rick Nowels, Charles Judge: synthesizer, George Black: synth bass, guitar, background vocals, Les Dudek, Michael Landau: guitar, Jamie Sherrif: synthesizer programming, Producer: Rick Nowels

Engineers: John Kovarek, Gabe Veltri, Robert Feist

4. 'I Sing For The Things' (Nicks)

Stevie Nicks: lead vocals, Sharon Celani, Lori Perry: background vocals, Russ Kunkel: drums

Danny Kortchmar: guitar, Benmont Tench: piano, Bob Glaub: bass, Bobbye Hall: percussion

Rick Nowels, Charles Judge: synthesizer

Producer: Jimmy Iovine, Engineer: Shelly Yakus

5. 'Imperial Hotel' (Nicks, Mike Campbell)

Stevie Nicks: lead vocals, Sharon Celani, Lori Perry, Marilyn Martin: background vocals, Mike Campbell: guitar, Benmont Tench: organ, Bob Glaub: bass, Steve Jordan: drums

Producers: Jimmy Iovine, Mike Campbell, Engineer: Gabe Veltri

6. 'Some Become Strangers' (David Williams, Amy Latelevision, Peter Rafelson)

Stevie Nicks: lead vocals, Sharon Celani, Lori Perry, Marilyn Martin: background vocals, Bob Glaub: bass, Greg Phillinganes: keyboards, Mike Landau: guitar, Steve Jordan: drums

Producer: Jimmy Iovine, Engineers: Gabe Veltri, Don Smith

Side Two:

1. 'Talk To Me' (Chas Sanford)

Stevie Nicks: lead vocals, Sharon Celani, Lori Perry, Maria Vidal: background vocals, Chas Sanford: drum machine, synthesizer, guitars, bass, Barney Wilens: saxophone, Greg Phillinganes: tympani

Producers: Chas Sanford, Jimmy Iovine, Engineers: Chas Sanford, Gabe Veltri

2. 'The Nightmare' (Nicks, Chris Nicks)

Stevie Nicks: lead vocals, synthesizer, Sharon Celani, Lori Perry, Maria Vidal:

background vocals, Charles Judge: synthesizer, George Black: synth bass, drums, vocals, Rick Nowels: synthesizer, background vocals, Mike Landau: guitars, Andy Newmark: drums, Producer: Rick Nowels, Engineers: John Kovarek, Gabe Veltri

3. 'If I Were You' (Nicks, Rick Nowels)
Stevie Nicks: lead vocals, Sharon Celani, Lori Perry: background vocals, Charles Judge: synthesizer, Mike Landau: guitar, Rick Nowels: guitar, background vocals, Andy Newmark: drums, David Kemper: tambourine
Producer: Rick Nowels, Engineers: John Kovarek, Gary Skardina, Robert Feist

4. 'No Spoken Word' (Nicks)
Stevie Nicks: lead vocals, Sharon Celani, Lori Perry, Marilyn Martin, Rick Nowels: background vocals, Waddy Wachtel: guitar, Denny Carmassi: drums, Bill Cuomo: keyboards, Mike Porcaro: bass, Producer: Keith Olsen, Engineers: Brian Foraker, Dennis Sager

5. 'Has Anyone Ever Written Anything For You?' (Nicks, Keith Olsen)
Stevie Nicks: lead vocals, Lori Perry, Carol Brooks: backing vocals, Charles Judge: keyboards, Jamie Sherrif: synthesizer programming, Mike Landau: guitar, David Kemper: percussion, Producer: Rick Nowels, Engineer: John Kovarek
Release Date: 18 November 1985
Chart places: US: 12, UK: 30
Running Time: 44:47

The contrast between *Rock a Little* and Stevie Nicks' previous solo albums was obvious from the opening track 'I Can't Wait'. Instead of the graceful arrangements of *Bella Donna* and *The Wild Heart*'s title songs, 'I Can't Wait' begins with a jittery rush of processed vocals, synthesizers and electronic drums. However, aside from an instrumental break reminiscent of New Order, once the song gets underway, Nicks' vocal personality asserts itself with lyrics that invert the sentiments of 'The Wild Heart'.

> She dances around in a circle
> Well she's got that feeling now
> Blame it on something at first sight
> Put the blame on me if you want to
> To be continued

Like most of Nicks' songs on the album, 'I Can't Wait' was a collaboration. She wrote in the liner notes for *Crystal Visions*: 'My longtime friend Rick Nowels originally sent me the track, hoping I would write a song to it. The very first time I sang the vocal is the one that's actually on the record. No way could I ever sing this song better than that first go 'round.' While this sentiment didn't keep her from performing the song in most shows of the *Rock a Little* tour, she's seldom played it live since 1986, despite it being one of her bigger solo hits.

While the title track 'Rock A Little (Go Ahead Lily)' sounds truer to form musically than 'I Can't Wait,' that isn't necessarily a positive. The restrained soundscape punctuated by Waddy Wachtel's playing (one of just two appearances on *Rock a Little*) is preferable to some of the more-labored arrangements elsewhere on the record, but the meandering lyric leaves it without a center of gravity.

> She's home now
> She says I've gone far beyond that song
> She says rock and roll ballerina
> Where else would she go?
> He knows his daughter, says
> 'Where does she live?'
> He says, 'Oh, up there somewhere'

'Sister Honey' features one of Nicks' best performances on the album, matched with a backing track that evokes the Minneapolis sound prevalent in the work of Prince and many of the artists in his orbit from the early-to-mid-1980s. With the song's co-writer being Les Dudek – a singer-songwriter whose other gigs included The Steve Miller Band, The Allman Brothers Band and Cher – that approach seems more a production choice than a compositional one. That said, despite some distracting sonic ephemera, the production complements her vocal rather than camouflaging it.

> Nobody's right baby
> All the time
> And a fool never knows what he's leaving behind

'I Sing For The Things' is a holdover from *The Wild Heart*, presented here in a revamped version. As a declaration that 'success-hasn't-spoiled-me-yet', it might've fit more naturally on the earlier record. Nevertheless, while it's hard to take lines like 'I'll take off my cape for you' seriously in this context, she sounds undeniably earnest.

You say I have everything
Well, I've been living on dreams and chains
I sing for the things money can't buy me

Like Waddy Wachtel, keyboardist Benmont Tench was a key player on Nicks' first two solo albums, whose presence on the third was significantly diminished. Not surprisingly, the two tracks he plays on – 'I Sing For the Things' and 'Imperial Hotel' – are the most musically aligned with the earlier records. Though Tom Petty himself wasn't on hand, Heartbreakers guitarist Mike Campbell – who co-wrote and co-produced 'Imperial Hotel' – helped bring Petty's sound to the album.

She sits across the table, the same glass table
Cries to her friend, 'Why am I so alone?'
He says, 'Who baby, baby, baby, baby
This is the path you have chosen'
She probably goes under another name
Well, that's a good idea

The final song on side one – 'Some Become Strangers' – is a great title for a Stevie Nicks song, but wasn't written by her and could've been performed just as well by any number of singers. The most interesting part of the song – the semi-spoken declaration 'I don't really need this in my life' – sounds like it was ported over from another song. While Iovine is credited as producer, the bland backing track suggests either a typo in the liner notes, or that he didn't want to fight with Nicks about its sound. In an interesting coincidence, one of the song's composers – Peter Rafelson, who also co-wrote Madonna's 1987 hit 'Open Your Heart' – co-produced Irish band The Corrs' 1998 cover of 'Dreams. Recorded for *Legacy: A Tribute to Fleetwood Mac's Rumours* (other contributors to which included Elton John and The Cranberries), The Corrs' rendition reached number 6 in the UK and Ireland.

Side two begins with one of Nicks' biggest solo hits – 'Talk to Me': the album's other song not written by her. In a commentary for the song's music video, she described Jimmy Iovine bringing the song to her as part of his effort to look out for potential hits, and recognizing it as a very commercial song herself: 'As good of a writer as I am – and I think I'm a pretty good writer – I have never been a real single writer. And if I do write a single, it's an accident.' The song's commercial success is unsurprising considering its close DNA match with 'Missing You' – the worldwide hit for John Waite that Chas Sanford wrote with Waite and Mark Leonard (who worked on actor Don Johnson's 1986 album *Heartbeat*). 'Talk To Me' features the same chugging synthesizers, and adds a prototypical 1980s saxophone solo. In her music-video commentary, Nicks referred to it as 'Jim Keltner's song,' in appreciation of the legendary drummer serving as the audience when she was struggling to get the vocal right. For all her effort, though, the song somehow manages to sound both overwrought and dispassionate.

> Oh, let the walls burn down
> Set your secrets free
> You can break their bounds
> 'Cause you're safe with me
> You can lose your doubt
> 'Cause you'll find no danger, not here

The next two songs – 'The Nightmare' and 'If I Were You' – were co-writes. Nicks wrote the former with her brother Chris, who also married her longstanding backing singer Lori Perry. The latter was written with Rick Nowels. More than anything on the album, 'If I Were You' illustrates the album's shortcomings. On Nicks' previous albums, even the weaker songs felt lived-in, but 'If I Were You' is just words: and pretentious ones at that.

> Well, I believe that love is a living thing
> Born into our destinies
> From a single moment of inspiration
> And as it grows, it changes your life forever

The final two songs would've been average on either of Nicks' previous solo albums, but on *Rock a Little,* they were highlights, closing the album on a positive note. Both reunited her with Keith Olsen, who produced the *Buckingham Nicks* album and the 1975 *Fleetwood Mac* album. He produced 'No Spoken Word' and co-wrote the final song 'Has Anyone Ever Written Anything For You?' with Nicks. That song went under the radar when released as a single, but has gained significant stature within Nicks' work. Between performances on her own and with Fleetwood Mac, it's the *Rock a Little* song she's played live most often, and the one to which she seems to have the deepest connection. Like so many of her songs, there was an emotional story behind it. As she related to interviewer James McNair in 2013, the subject wasn't her own life but rather that of Joe Walsh and his daughter Emma Kristen, who died when she was three. Nicks and Walsh began a romantic relationship that stayed largely under the radar during the tour for *The Wild Heart*. When the tour was scheduled to play in Denver, Colorado, Walsh took her to the nearby city of Boulder and showed her a memorial to Emma.

> (Joe) told me the whole story about how Emma had been killed by a drunk driver on the way to nursery school. Joe had been married to a woman named Stephanie, but they couldn't survive what had happened, and they broke up. My song was for Stephanie too, I think. It was for all of us, actually. It was about the whole tragic story and how the stupidity of some drunk asshole driving into a Porsche, tore so many lives apart.

The relationship with Walsh ended suddenly in 1984, for reasons Nicks said she never understood, but he performed on one of the songs recorded for *Rock a Little* that didn't make the final album. 'One More Big Time Rock And Roll Star' was released as the B-side of 'Talk To Me'.

Rock a Little hasn't received a deluxe reissue like its predecessors, but at least one noteworthy outtake has been released: Nicks' rendition of Warren Zevon's 'Reconsider Me.' Despite being better-known for offbeat compositions such as 'Poor Poor Pitiful Me' and 'Werewolves Of London,' the late singer-songwriter had a remarkable gift for tender and thoughtful love songs. Zevon's version of 'Reconsider Me' was released on his 1987 album *Sentimental Hygiene* – his first after a long hiatus – while Nicks' version surfaced in the 1998 box set *Enchanted*. Passing over such a distinctive song in favor of anonymous compositions like 'If I Were You' or 'Some Become Strangers,' exemplifies the questionable choices that made *Rock a Little* so uneven. Nicks hinted at some retrospective misgivings in the *Enchanted* liner notes: 'Jimmy Iovine brought me this song written by Warren Zevon. I think Jimmy and I were fighting, and for some reason, I wasn't in a very 'reconsider me' state of mind. I don't think Jimmy ever forgave me for not trusting his judgment. So, Jimmy, here it is, little one. Better late than never. And yes, Don Henley *is* singing with me. (And Warren, thank you.)'

The other Fleetwood Mac members were also musically active in 1985. Lindsey Buckingham and Christine McVie contributed to a new album by Walter Egan, performing on various tracks and co-writing a couple of songs with him. The record – which included his version of Nicks' 'Sisters Of The Moon' with Annie McLoone on vocals – fell victim to label politics, and wasn't released until 2000.

Buckingham and McVie also worked on projects of their own – one of which had somewhat surprising results. Among the lesser-known highlights of Buckingham's 2018 solo retrospective was 'Time Bomb Town', which he recorded for the soundtrack to the 1985 movie *Back to the Future*. Discussing his 1980s soundtrack work on Stereogum, Buckingham acknowledged the making of 'Holiday Road' as a case where he perceived 'the stakes are quite low.' 'Time Bomb Town' – which he described as 'just kind of a goof' that 'was buried somewhere behind some scene in a movie' – never attained the same following, but he saw its virtues nevertheless. 'I knew it was good. I loved the chord changes in it. I hadn't heard it in so long, and when I got back and listened to it again, I was really surprised at how well it held up.'

Christine McVie recording an Elvis Presley cover for the soundtrack of Blake Edwards' movie *A Fine Mess* could also have been perceived as low stakes but was ultimately the catalyst for something more impactful. Knowing that Buckingham was an Elvis fan, Richard Dashut suggested McVie ask him to play on her version of 'Can't Help Falling In Love.' The addition of Mick Fleetwood and John McVie made this August 1985 recording the largest musical gathering of Fleetwood Mac members since their performance on *Top of the Pops* in early 1983. The end result went well beyond an enjoyable rendition of a classic song. McVie said in 1987: 'The atmosphere in the studio was so instant, we jammed for hours and played some of the old songs. At that point, we sat down and said let's get serious about the studio again.'

Fleetwood recalled in his second autobiography: 'I don't think any of us, besides me, showed up thinking about making another Fleetwood Mac record. But once we were in the same room, how couldn't we?'

1986: That House on the Hill

'I never want to spend a year in the studio again to make one record.'
Christine McVie's sentiment, expressed in the press kit for her 1984 album,
would've been a rational expectation for most bands, but her hope was
misplaced. Fleetwood Mac's next album *Tango in the Night* took well over
a year to finish, in part because the band had difficulty agreeing on how to
start. Even getting all the members to agree to work on a new album, was
difficult now that the band was no longer managed internally, with one of
the five especially reluctant to put aside their solo work. Christine and John
McVie came on board quickly, as did Stevie Nicks, albeit with the others
needing to work around her individual commitments. 'Lindsey Buckingham
alone was fairly reticent,' wrote Fleetwood in his earlier autobiography.

The guitarist was working on his third solo album, and was not eager
to immerse himself in the band's personal and musical politics again. He
relented because, as Fleetwood explained, 'We worked to build enough
momentum, that we were able to convince Lindsey that it might go off
without him.' To ease the pressure on Buckingham – who'd taken on
a greater role in producing the group's records since *Rumours* – they
decided to work with an outside producer. However, this was a well-
intentioned idea that ultimately complicated matters.

After the band determined that Chic's Nile Rodgers (whose production
work ranged from David Bowie to Diana Ross) wasn't a fit, Warner Bros.
Records CEO Mo Ostin encouraged them to try Jason Corsaro. Corsaro
had established a good reputation as an engineer, working on the Duran
Duran side project The Power Station, who were produced by Rodgers'
musical partner from Chic: Bernard Edwards. Corsaro then co-produced
Duran Duran's James Bond theme 'A View To A Kill' with Edwards.
Though neither project suggested a particular affinity for Fleetwood
Mac's musical approach, the band kept an open mind.

While Stevie Nicks was in Australia hanging out with Bob Dylan and
Tom Petty and the Heartbreakers during their True Confessions tour,
the rest of the group held what Fleetwood termed 'a week of glorified
rehearsals.' This effort was unproductive musically but helped them
understand that an outside producer was the wrong fit for Fleetwood
Mac. Mick explained: 'It took us about a week to realize that any outside
producer who tried to harness the old Mac at this point was going to be
in way over his head. So Mr. Corsaro went home, and for a while in early
1986 it looked as if this record wasn't going to get made.'

Considering how events later unfolded, their path forward was ironic. Buckingham told *Creem* magazine: 'Richard Dashut and I were about halfway through my solo album, and the needs of the many started to outweigh the needs of the few.' Having initially hoped to quickly finish his contributions to the Fleetwood Mac album and return his focus to his own record, circumstances dictated putting the solo work aside to focus on the band. Buckingham attributed the decision, not just to the shared recognition that Corsaro 'didn't know how to handle us salty old guys,' but also the realization that 'If we were going to do it all, it just wasn't our style to go in half-assed and be part of something that was piecemealed together.'

Despite those good intentions, the group still had to work around Stevie Nicks. Unlike the *Mirage* sessions – where she limited her promotional efforts for *Bella Donna* to help the band finish that album – in 1986, her solo career took precedence. With 'I Can't Wait' hitting its peak on the US charts, Nicks kicked off her tour for *Rock a Little* in Houston, Texas. As on her previous tour, she chose a 1970s guitar legend as her opening act. Though there's no indication of anything but a professional relationship between Nicks and Peter Frampton, him being the opening act was not without significance.

A decade earlier, while the band were promoting *Fleetwood Mac*, they played at iconic concert promoter Bill Graham's Day on the Green event in Oakland, California, where Peter Frampton was the headliner. After years of records that went under the radar, both Frampton and Fleetwood Mac achieved massive commercial breakthroughs in 1976. However, while the band's popularity endured into the 1980s, Frampton was unable to sustain the success of *Frampton Comes Alive*, and the tour with Nicks was in support of his would-be comeback album *Premonition*.

Her August show at the famed Red Rocks amphitheater near Denver, Colorado, was recorded for the 1987 concert video *Live at Red Rocks*. Despite being an unremarkable example of the format (aside from some onstage hijinks involving a white dove), the 1987 release was nominated for a Grammy award in the newly established category of Best Performance Music Video: losing to U2's video for 'Where The Streets Have No Name.' Like Peter Frampton, Mick Fleetwood was promoted as a special guest on the video. Fleetwood's instrumental involvement was relatively limited, but his presence gave him an up-close look at the impact drugs and drinking were having on his friend.

Nicks was quite aware of this situation, and had resolved to deal with it before the tour started. As she told *Performing Songwriter* in 2007: 'I had already booked this seven-month tour, but I knew that the second the tour was over in October, that I would be going straight into the Betty Ford Center.' She also recalled the decision being sparked by a plastic surgeon who warned that the damage cocaine use had caused to her nose, could lead to a fatal brain hemorrhage. Nevertheless, she persisted in her efforts to balance her various commitments: 'I was terrified. But I wasn't going to cancel my tour, so I decided I was just going to walk a tightrope for the next six months. And I did. I took as good care of myself as I could, and I did as little of that stuff as I could possibly do to get through it.'

The *Rock a Little* tour ended with a series of shows in Australia – the last of which was a 6 October concert at the Sydney Entertainment Centre. This was the same venue where Nicks ran afoul of local authorities earlier in the year by singing 'Knockin' On Heaven's Door' with Bob Dylan and Tom Petty when she didn't have a visa allowing her to work in the country. When warned she faced a permanent ban on performing in Australia, she'd stopped appearing there onstage with Dylan and Petty, but not before adding backing vocals when they recorded the title song of the mostly forgotten movie *Band of the Hand* at a local studio.

After the tour, Nicks followed through on her commitment to seek treatment for her cocaine addiction at the Betty Ford Center. Virtually synonymous with addiction treatment, the Southern California facility was named for the former US First Lady who helped found it in 1982. Nicks likened the program there to a military boot camp, but was satisfied with the results, which she credited with saving her life. She told Uncut in 2003: 'I haven't even seen cocaine since 1986. Nobody would ever take it out in front of me, because they know I would call the police.'

Unfortunately, pressure from friends who were worried that Nicks might relapse, led to her swapping one addiction for another for several years. 'I don't hate anyone, but I *hate* him,' said Nicks of the psychiatrist who prescribed the tranquilizer Klonopin that left her feeling mentally foggy when the time finally came to rejoin Fleetwood Mac in the studio. In a 2007 interview with Sylvie Simmons, she described the psychiatrist as a 'rock star groupie' and even worse than cocaine dealers who she saw as just trying to get by: 'This guy was rich and had no reason except that he wanted to keep me coming to his office a couple times and tell him about what was going on in Hollywood.'

As for the rest of the band, Lindsey Buckingham agreeing to produce the new album in tandem with Richard Dashut might've solved one problem, but it also set the stage for several more. Nicks' diminished presence would've been difficult enough, but when gathering at Rumbo Recorders to record the album's basic tracks, some of the other members presented challenges. According to Mick Fleetwood, two years of infrequent playing had left John McVie lacking in confidence: 'I could tell John was suffering a serious artistic block; a blind panic of the kind I used to feel when they asked me questions at school.' Though McVie's slow going worried the other band members and drinking was still a concern, Mick's encouragement helped McVie work through those difficulties and 'get his chops back.'

The drummer's compassion for his longtime friend and musical partner isn't surprising but is still remarkable in the context of Mick's own ongoing substance-abuse issues: 'It is absolutely safe to say that at that moment in our history, Stevie and I were at the top of the list of Fleetwood Mac members who needed to make lifestyle changes that had nothing to do with music, and make them quick.' Mick's comments from the liner notes of the 2017 deluxe edition of *Tango in the Night* echoed an observation Lindsey Buckingham made in the 2003 *Uncut* article 'Five Go Mad': 'Everyone was at their worst, including myself. We'd made the progression from what could be seen as an acceptable or excusable amount of drug use to a situation where we had all hit the wall. I think of it as our darkest period.'

After the initial sessions at Rumbo, production of *Tango in the Night* moved to Buckingham's home studio The Slope. In his second autobiography, Mick noted that while this was ostensibly for overdubs and mixing, The Slope 'was the nexus of where that album was made.' Refining songs after their initial recording sessions, had become a Fleetwood Mac tradition – the impact of which was well-documented in the deluxe editions of *Rumours, Tusk* and *Mirage*. In this instance, for Buckingham and Richard Dashut, the task proved to be much more complex. The former found himself with a level of creative control over the band's sound that he hadn't had since *Tusk*.

To maintain some distance between band-driven craziness and the more-stable environment the guitarist was seeking, the group set up a trailer outside his house to serve as a recreational space for those inclined to indulge. He told *Guitar World*'s Alan di Perna in 1997: 'Everyone was up at the house. We had a Winnebago parked in the driveway. It was a major scene up there.'

Mick Fleetwood later reflected on the irony that being in a rock band had become the boring part of his life. Although, he also acknowledged the upside of '(becoming) a fly on the wall watching a brilliant mad scientist working in his laboratory.' Buckingham described it in the *Tango in the Night* liner notes: 'So, there was this collective insanity going on within the band, that on one level made it difficult to get things done, yet on another level, that left me and our co-producer Richard Dashut and our engineer Greg Droman, a little more in charge of the day-to-day recording process. In a strange way, that worked in our favor, because a lot of the stuff on *Tango In The Night* holds up well.'

1987 – This Is a Dream, Right?

In the liner notes for the *Tango in the Night* deluxe edition, Lindsey Buckingham said: 'Stevie was pretty much disconnected from our band, and off in her own world. Out of what was probably a year of work on the album, we saw Stevie for, at the most, a couple of weeks.'

Untangling coincidence and causation is tricky with Fleetwood Mac, because, frequently there are multiple factors driving any given event. Stevie Nicks' touring commitments and going into rehab, played obvious roles in limiting her involvement with the album. However, even post-rehab, when she rejoined the group at The Slope in January 1987, she still kept some distance from the record. Viewed in retrospect – as it wasn't widely known at the time – her new dependency issue with Klonopin was part of the problem. But the bigger issue was one that had been in place for over a decade, and arguably remains unresolved in 2022. In his 1990 autobiography, Mick Fleetwood described Nicks as 'dreading' going into the studio with Lindsey Buckingham, due to her being anxious that he'd be unpleasant and dictatorial with her. Nicks' comments in articles around the time of the *Tango In The Night* release point to deeper animosity toward her former partner. In the *Creem* article 'Return Without Leaving,' Nicks bristled when asked about her level of involvement:

> Lindsey was doing another solo album too. If he hadn't been Lindsey – if he'd been me – then he could've gone ahead and done his at the same time Fleetwood Mac was doing theirs. But Lindsey having to be the boss – and pretty much the head of this particular tribe at this particular moment – he couldn't do both. I could, because there wasn't all that much for me to do, in the technical sense, at the beginning of the record.

Even allowing for the enduring bruised feelings between them, Nicks' remarks seem unfair toward Buckingham. Whatever reluctance he initially displayed about returning to the band, choosing to not just put his own record on hold, but give several of its songs-in-progress *to the band,* represented both a personal and artistic sacrifice. Mick acknowledged this in his second autobiography: 'It was entirely his choice to come back and do *Tango.* And looking back, it was a huge gesture for him; much bigger than any of us realized at the time.'

Nicks expressed deeper discontent with Buckingham in a *BAM* article later in 1987, after Fleetwood Mac announced their tour for the album:

Lindsey 'would rather I just stayed at home doing laundry. We're talking about a man who was in love with a woman and would just as soon she'd faded out and just been his old lady or wife. Period.' As forthright as her comments seem, here again, it's difficult to reconcile them with some basic facts – namely, the guitarist's insistence upon being asked to join the band, that he and Nicks came as a package.

All that said, Nicks' reticence about recording in her ex-boyfriend's home was understandable. In the album liner notes, she recalled: 'The vocals were being done right in their master bedroom, and as out-of-it as I may have been then, even I knew that was *weird*.' In March 2017, she elaborated on this in an interview with Howard Cohen for the *Miami Herald*: 'In all fairness, it was like the only empty room, and they had a beautiful master bedroom all set up like a vocal booth, but I found it very uncomfortable, personally. I guess I didn't go very often, and when I did go, I would get like, 'Give me a shot of brandy and let me sing on four or five songs off the top of my head'.' Nicks conceded that, 'Vocals done when you're crazy and drinking a cup of brandy, probably aren't usually going to be great,' and didn't blame Buckingham – the studio perfectionist – for not using many of them on the final versions. As he told *Guitar World* interviewer Alan di Perna in 1997, *Tango In The Night* 'took close to a year to make, and I think we saw Stevie for about three weeks out of that time. And these weeks weren't the greatest three weeks.'

Buckingham had a more-productive dynamic with Christine McVie. In addition to being one of his fellow studio junkies, she worked with him on several songs, three of which appeared on the album. Not counting B-sides and outtakes, the guitarist had a writing credit on seven of the album's 12 tracks, though that still understates his contribution. McVie told *BAM* magazine: 'Lindsey and Richard were at the fore, without question, when it came to the ideas and the sound and the production. Of course, one has to say, *nothing* went on the album that the rest of us didn't like.'

McVie's insistence notwithstanding, the disconnected state of the band meant that Buckingham and Dashut's job wasn't just to shape the album's sound and style, but on a more basic level make it sound like a band effort in the first place. Buckingham explained in the album's liner notes: 'At times, we would have to channel Stevie when she wasn't there because she's obviously such an important part of the Fleetwood Mac sound. So Christine and I would sing and speed things up and slow things down and use that kind of trickery to summon her spirit.' That trickery – as he related in 1997 – also extended to the material Nicks actually recorded:

'We just did whatever we could, really. We had to take little bits of Stevie singing off-the-cuff and make a whole vocal track out of that because that's all we'd get out of her.' To accomplish this, the Fairlight CMI – which he'd found so useful on *Go Insane* – once again became an invaluable tool 'to make up for a natural interplay of musicians that wasn't really there.'

For the *New York Times* review of the album, Buckingham told Stephen Holden: 'Most of the vocal parts were recorded track-by-track. The voices used in the textured vocal choirs were mostly mine. I used a Fairlight machine that samples real sounds and blends them orchestrally. Constructing such elaborate layering is a lot like painting a canvas, and is best done in solitude.'

Though co-producer Richard Dashut recognized the personal difficulties at work within the band, in a 2017 *Salon* article about the album's making, he expressed mixed feelings about Buckingham's preferred approach and the band's overall lack of participation as a cohesive unit:

I loved, sonically, what it was doing. But I started to miss the old live feeling of the band. Not that we did that with any of the albums live; they were all overdubbed. But still, it all started off with the band in the studio playing together, as did *Tango*, although not so much. But I think the Fairlight started replacing some of that human touch: some of the other band members. Lindsey was able to do a lot more on his own and control it a lot more artistically.

For all the challenges that making the album posed, Buckingham still found a creative upside in it. Many of his comments after rejoining Fleetwood Mac reflected an appreciation of the opportunities offered by working with 'the big machine' – as he sometimes called the band – relative to 'the small machine' of his solo career. He commented in the album's 2017 edition liner notes: 'Looking back, I feel like after doing my solo album *Go Insane*, in 1984, I was able to bring some of the experimentation I longed for back into Fleetwood Mac on *Tango In The Night*. So even if I couldn't paint musical paintings as I wished like on *Tusk*, I was able to assert a certain level of control now that I was slightly out of the penalty box with the rest of the band.'

Buckingham's meticulous approach extended to mixing the album. Engineer Greg Droman told *Salon*: 'We would take easily a week to mix a song. Sometimes we'd mix a song, and Lindsey would think of another part he wanted to put on, and we'd start the whole thing all over again.'

Richard Dashut acknowledged: 'He was tough to work with. He could be brash; he could be harsh. He was very motivated. He always kept his eye on the prize: which is about quality music.'

Despite the complicated atmosphere around *Tango In The Night* and the aftermath of its release, one party who agreed with Dashut's assessment, was Stevie Nicks: 'I absolutely love *Tango In The Night*, and with this album, I can say that with a certain amount of objectivity, because the truth is I wasn't even around for very much of it.' In the album's 2017 liner notes, she added, 'In terms of Lindsey's songs, *Tango In The Night* is my favorite Fleetwood Mac record ever, so I do give credit where credit is due.'

Whether or not most record buyers completely agreed with Nicks, the public enthusiastically embraced *Tango In The Night,* and made its first single, 'Big Love' a top ten hit in the US and UK. With sales estimated at over 15,000,000, the album is second only to *Rumours* among their albums and was especially popular in the UK, reaching number one on three separate occasions during an almost two-year run on the album chart. Like *Rumours*, it benefited from a series of strong singles – four making the US top 20 – and a trio of UK top-10 appearances.

For the most part, contemporary and retrospective reviews were favorable. *Rolling Stone* writer Jon Pareles' 1987 review praised *Tango On The Night* for showing 'how passion swirls behind the neatest of facades', while, in 2017, *The Guardian*'s Alexis Petridis found it 'even more deserving of the *flawed-masterpiece* tag than *Tusk*.' Robert Christgau's *Village Voice* review damned the record with faint praise, describing it as 'marginally better' than *Mirage*. However, while his snark sometimes feels self-conscious, it holds up better than many 1987 reviews in one key respect: the treatment of Stevie Nicks.

Even considering the relative weakness of her contributions to *Tango In The Night*, some of the criticisms leveled at the time feel needlessly personal. In an otherwise thoughtful review in the *Los Angeles Times*, Steve Hochman wrote: 'Predictably, the album's lesser moments come courtesy of Nicks, who on the obtuse 'Welcome To The Room... Sara,' furthers her reputation as the Shirley MacLaine of rock.' Jon Pareles and Stephen Holden likewise unloaded on that song – a critique which seems all the more wrongheaded, directed as it was at one of the album's most deeply-felt tracks. Giving Hochman the benefit of the doubt that he declined to give Stevie Nicks, he was at least right to praise the album for combining the experimentation of 1979's *Tusk* and 'the crisp pop sense of 1977's multi-multi-million-selling *Rumours*.'

Tango In The Night (1987)

Personnel:

Lindsey Buckingham: vocals, guitar, keyboards, Fairlight CMI, bass, lap harp, percussion, synthesizer, drum programming

Mick Fleetwood: drums, percussion

Christine McVie: vocals, keyboards, synthesizer

John McVie: bass

Stevie Nicks: vocals

Producers: Lindsey Buckingham, Richard Dashut

Arranger: Lindsey Buckingham

Engineer: Greg Droman

Release Date: 13 April 1987

Chart places: US: 7, UK: 1

Running Time: 44:28

Side One: 1. 'Big Love' (Buckingham), 2. 'Seven Wonders' (Nicks, Sandy Stewart), 3. 'Everywhere' (Christine McVie), 4. 'Caroline' (Buckingham), 5. 'Tango In The Night' (Buckingham), 6. 'Mystified' (McVie, Buckingham)

Side Two: 1. 'Little Lies' (McVie, Eddy Quintela), 2. 'Family Man' (Buckingham, Richard Dashut), 3. 'Welcome To The Room... Sara' (Nicks), 4. 'Isn't It Midnight' (McVie, Quintela, Buckingham), 5. 'When I See You Again' (Nicks), 6 'You And I, Part II' (Buckingham, McVie)

2017 Reissue Bonus Disc:

1. 'Down Endless Street' (Buckingham), 2. 'Special Kind Of Love' (Buckingham), 3. 'Seven Wonders' (Early version) (Stewart, Nicks), 4. 'Tango In The Night' (Demo) (Buckingham), 5. 'Mystified' (Alternate version) (McVie, Buckingham), 6. 'Book Of Miracles' (Instrumental) (Buckingham, Nicks), 7. 'Where We Belong' (Demo) (Buckingham, McVie), 8. 'Ricky' (McVie, Buckingham), 9. 'Juliet' (Run-through) (Buckingham, Nicks), 10. 'Isn't It Midnight' (Alternate mix) (McVie, Quintela, Buckingham), 11. 'Ooh My Love' (Buckingham), 12. 'Mystified' (Instrumental demo) (McVie, Buckingham), 13. 'You And I, Part I & II' (Full version) (Buckingham, McVie)

While Christine McVie was Fleetwood Mac's most reliable writer of hit singles in the 1970s and 1980s, Lindsey Buckingham songs were lead-off singles for more of the band's albums than either of his fellow writers. 'Big Love' – which was among the tracks originally intended for his solo album – was the last of these. Echoes of its guitar figure can be heard in 'Doing What I Can' from Buckingham's 1992 album *Out Of The Cradle*.

You said that you love me
And that you always will
Oh you begged me to keep you
In that house on the hill

The single's release was accompanied by tabloid-level speculation about who provided the passionate sounds throughout the song. Much to her chagrin, some speculated that the voice was Buckingham's girlfriend. And – perhaps inevitably – Stevie Nicks also became part of the discussion. The truth turned out to be far less scandalous. Buckingham had sampled his voice and altered it to sound like a woman.

One upside of the solo rendition he started performing on his 1992 tour and continued playing after rejoining Fleetwood Mac, is how it sidestepped the need to duplicate those sounds or any other element of its intricate production.

In Buckingham's 2003 interview in *Performing Songwriter*, he also described how this approach enables him to express his musical style in a more fundamental way: 'I started doing 'Big Love' very fast, in a Leo Kottke-meets-classical on acid, whatever you want to call it. It got such a strong response, and it got me back to reminding myself that whatever I can do as a producer, this is the center of what I do, and it's not something to be taken lightly.'

The second track 'Seven Wonders' was also the album's second single, and the only Stevie song from it to be released as a single. Though UK listeners seemed less impressed (based on it stalling outside the top 50), it reached the top 20 in the US. The catchy song was primarily written by Sandy Stewart. However, Nicks apparently misheard the line 'All the way down you held the line,' and her alternate lyric took hold. She told *The Miami Herald*: 'I was so used to saying, 'All the way down to Emmiline,' so we used that. 'I asked Sandy, a really good friend of mine, and she said 'Fine.' It totally created a character.' It's a testament to the strength of Nicks' personality that such a small change makes a song sound indelibly her own. The song had a second life in 2014 – charting again in the US after being featured in the season finale of *American Horror Story: Coven*.

All the way back you held out your hand
If I hope and if I pray
Ooh it might work out someday

Christine McVie's only solo-written song on the album – 'Everywhere' – also reached the US top 20, and fared even better in the UK, where it peaked at 4. Mick Fleetwood recalled that the song 'glistened like gemstone, even in Chris' original demo.' With enveloping vocal harmonies and just the right degree of instrumental ornamentation, the track represents an ideal fusion between McVie's compositional style and Buckingham's production sensibilities.

> I'll speak a little louder
> I'll even shout
> You know that I'm proud
> And I can't get the words out

Like 'Seven Wonders,' 'Everywhere' also enjoyed a second life, hitting the UK top 20 in 2013 after being used in an advertisement. More recently, singers Niall Horan and Anne-Marie recorded a version of it to support the BBC's 2021 Children In Need campaign. 'I'm thrilled with this new version of 'Everywhere' and to be part of this year's Children in Need campaign,' said McVie of their rendition, which charted in the UK, Ireland and New Zealand. 'I hope we can really make a difference.'

The next two songs – 'Caroline' and 'Tango In The Night' – each encapsulate extremes of Lindsey Buckingham's musical style. Another song originally intended for his third solo album, 'Caroline' is less inventive than his other songs on the album, but nevertheless improves on the approach of *Go Insane*'s 'Play In The Rain.'

> Time recedes with a fatal drop
> Dusty fury on the mountaintop
> Cut the cord if you can

With excellent guitar work, the title track offers a more dynamic expression of desire in a similar vein to 'Big Love,' if not as catchy. Mick Fleetwood recounted the track as evolving out of 'a two-piece drunken transcension between Lindsey and me,' using the older song 'I'm So Afraid' as a springboard.

Mick identified this as a rare moment of extracurricular indulgence on Buckingham's part while making the album – seemingly from its early stages, when he was still trying to balance the group project and his solo record.

Then I remember
When the moon was full and bright
I would take you in the darkness
And do the tango in the night

Christine McVie songs close side one and begin side two. While not so different lyrically or melodically from her compositions on previous records, the production creates a world around them. That sonic approach holds true for most of the album. But with McVie being the most stable and proficient songwriter, her work arguably benefits the most. Like the two Buckingham songs preceding them, this pair exemplify different avenues of McVie's songwriting. 'Mystified' has a wistful feel akin to *Mirage*'s 'Wish You Were Here,' or 'The Smile I Live For' from her 1984 solo record.

There's a magic surrounds you
Tell me where your secret lies

In turn, 'Little Lies' is this album's sleekest pop song. The synthesizer and vocal hooks made it an obvious choice for a single, and it became one of the band's biggest hits, reaching the top 5 in the US and UK, and the top ten in several European countries. Intentional or not, the lyric also feels like a commentary on the band itself.

No more broken hearts
We're better off apart
Let's give it a try
Tell me, tell me, tell me lies

'Family Man' – a Buckingham/Dashut co-wrote – is mildly catchy but still a surprising choice for a single – especially one released after the guitarist's departure. Though it didn't do much on the charts, the release was noteworthy for including the Buckingham-composed non-album track 'Down Endless Street' as its B-side, and for an unusual music video.

Aside from a narrative video for 'Everywhere' by *Dark City* director Alex Proyas, the music videos for *Tango In The Night* emphasized the band performing, complemented by flourishes such as the visual recursion in 'Big Love.' However, the truncated clip for 'Family Man,'

Frankenstein-ed band footage from the 'Seven Wonders' video with archival footage of families in various historical settings.

Walk down this road
When the road gets rough
I fall down
I get up

Stevie Nicks' most significant song on the album – 'Welcome To The Room... Sara' – was written about her experience at The Betty Ford Center the year before. Even without factoring in that background, the derision many critics directed at the track seems wrongheaded. While it's possible (even likely) that Nicks' vocal was assembled from a multitude of recorded efforts, it still comes across as her most assured performance on the album.

It's not home
And it's not Tara
In fact, do I know you?
Have I been here before?
This is a dream, right?
Déja vu
Did I come here on my own

While Nicks hasn't played 'Welcome To The Room...Sara' in her own concerts or with the band, she has explained the song's origins several times. In the 2017 liner notes for the album, she noted that she 'thought it was important to write about that experience, especially back then before rehab was talked about much by people.' That echoed her comments from the 1987 *Creem* article about the album, where she explicitly tied this song to the earlier 'Sara' and discussed her mindset in writing it: 'I don't really want anyone to know whether I'm going into her room or she's coming into mine, or what's in her room. This room is an ominous room. I'm not Bob Dylan, but every once in a while, I've gotta say something.'

Christine McVie's 'Isn't It Midnight' was the album's sixth and final single. Despite being typically confident and catchy, with strong interplay between guitars and keyboards, its muted reception in the United States and Britain suggests its release was probably a bridge too far.

So cool, calm and collected
You had a style, a rakish style
Well my poor heart never connected
You'd stay so long on my mind

Stevie Nicks' final song on the album – 'When I See You Again' – is a heartbreaking piece in the tradition of 'Landslide,' though not nearly as focused. Near the end, the song features a striking vocal Interjection from Lindsey Buckingham: added at Nicks' insistence. In *Creem* magazine, she discussed at length this rare but effective example of her directly influencing the record's production:

We went out and sang 'If I see you again, will it be over?' We sang it in unison, then I snuck in and took my voice off. Otherwise, I'd have never gotten him to do it. See, Lindsey's pretty shy, and he's singing differently there than he is on anything else on the record. He wouldn't think to do that – to sing on my song at the end. He would think to sing *with* me, but he wouldn't want to end it. But that's what I wanted – to leave people feeling they are really talking to each other.

If any band was ideally equipped to end an album on a note that was equal parts upbeat and anxious, it was this incarnation of Fleetwood Mac. The bouncy synths and ethereal harmonies of 'You and I, Part II,' perfectly complement lyrics balancing darkness and hope. While it's not Buckingham and McVie's best co-write, it's still a distinctive expression of their combined sensibilities.

Oh the phantoms crawl out of the night
Hoping the daylight will never come
For you and I

The album's 2017 deluxe edition included the full version of the song. While it was the first combined release of both parts, 'You and I, Part I' had already been released, as the B-side of 'Big Love.' The band's embrace of the singles format included a variety of remixes and extended versions, but after the long wait, the four non-album tracks were probably the most appreciated by fans. The reissue included these alongside some demos, additional outtakes and alternate versions. One aspect of previous Fleetwood Mac reissues that was conspicuously absent, was live performances from the tour that followed the album's initial release. Most likely, this is because the version of the band who toured to promote *Tango In The Night*, wasn't the same band that *made* it. Buckingham's departure shortly before the tour was scheduled to begin left the group with little choice but to continue without him. That said, recordings from those shows would've felt incongruous on a re-release intended to celebrate a musical achievement that owed so much to Lindsey Buckingham.

Buckingham's decision to leave the band, wasn't entirely surprising. Shortly after it was publicly announced, Christine McVie told *BAM*:

> We sensed this was probably the last thing Lindsey would do with us. It was sort of said, but not said, you know? He admitted his solo career was becoming his priority. But by the end of the album, he did sort of agree to tour, then at the eleventh hour, he just pulled out, saying that he simply couldn't cope with it.

McVie's account is less sensational than the one that appeared in Mick Fleetwood's initial autobiography. His recollection of the early-August meeting at Christine McVie's house that ended with Buckingham walking out, is filled with soap-opera-worthy moments:

> In interviews, Lindsey had been describing his role in the band as the grand interpreter of Chris' and Stevie's music to the world – as if he felt he had carried the rest of the band. Nobody liked this – especially now.

> Lindsey grabbed Stevie and slapped her and bent her backwards over the hood of his car. Was he going to hit her again? He'd done it before.

> There was a silence. And John McVie quietly said to Lindsey Buckingham, 'I think you'd better leave now.'

When interviewed for the debut episode of the 1995 BBC series *Rock Family Trees*, John McVie explained the latter comment as being intended simply to get Buckingham to back off and diffuse tensions, rather than to leave the group. He also described the situation as 'physically ugly,' and indicated that it got violent. However, Stevie Nicks' interview for the same program, adds further dimension to that physical confrontation: 'I flew out of the couch and across the room to seriously attack him,' said Nicks, adding that the fight boiled over outside the house. 'I thought he was going to kill me, and I think he probably thought that he was going to kill me too.'

While acknowledging the unpleasantness of that day, Buckingham has disputed the specifics: 'There's something in (Mick's book) about me slapping Stevie, which never happened,' he told *Los Angeles Times* reviewer Nick Boehm in a 1992 interview for *Out of the Cradle*: Buckingham's first solo album after leaving Fleetwood Mac. It's telling that even with much catchier songs to draw from, the record's first single was 'Wrong' – a track widely believed to be a response to Mick's book.

Further clouding the question is Fleetwood's later autobiography. He describes himself and the rest of the band as being 'furious' with Buckingham for backing out of the tour on short notice after initially agreeing to go on the road but makes no mention of the guitarist reciprocating that fury. Considering the personalities involved, it's hard to believe there wasn't a physical fight between Buckingham and Nicks, but Fleetwood simply states that, 'Historically, that was not a happy day.'

Outside of the 1991 telling, Mick's comments have largely validated Buckingham's assertion that leaving the band rather than returning to the party atmosphere that touring would've entailed, was 'a survival move' on his part. Mick also recognized the musical and personal divergence between the guitarist and the group, in a 2001 interview with Sean Egan: 'He wanted to move on and do different things, and we had grown apart as people. He had a vision for his creative journey, and much like Peter Green didn't see it as part of Fleetwood Mac.' With the benefit of further hindsight, in 2017, Mick offered his most telling remark about the album and the events surrounding its genesis: 'Making *Tango In The Night*, and then falling apart before we could take it on the road – it's one of those many elements in the Fleetwood Mac story that could only be us.'

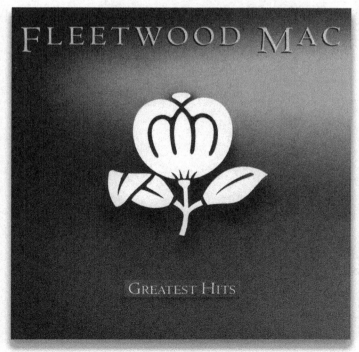

FLEETWOOD MAC   TANGO IN THE NIGHT

Right: 1987's *Tango in the Night* had a difficult genesis but became the band's second most popular album after *Rumours.* (*Warner Bros.*)

FLEETWOOD MAC

GREATEST HITS

Left: Two new songs on Fleetwood Mac's Greatest Hits were Billy Burnette and Rick Vito's first recordings with the group. (*Warner Bros.*)

Left: Like most of the videos for *Tango in the Night*, the clip for 'Seven Wonders' focused on the band performing.

Right: Though primarily written by her collaborator, Sandy Stewart, a misunderstanding of the lyrics led to Nicks receiving co-writing credit.

Left: 'Seven Wonders' reached the Top 20 in the US but was far less popular in the UK.

Right: *Tango in the Night's* third single, 'Little Lies', was another impeccable pop song from Christine Mcvie.

Left: Stevie Nicks was absent for much of *Tango in the Night's* production, but her vocals feature prominently in 'Little Lies.'

Right: Lindsey Buckingham had already left Fleetwood Mac by the time it reached the top ten in both the US and UK.

1988: As Long As You Follow

Of the many personnel changes in Fleetwood Mac's history, very few are as significant as Buckingham's 1987 departure. Only the exits of Peter Green and Bob Welch – the latter of which set the stage for Buckingham and Nicks to join the band – seem comparable in terms of shifting the band's sound. Buckingham leaving, arguably had an even-greater impact, because the change that ensued went beyond their musical identity.

Carrying on with new musicians – as the band did in 1987 – had the unusual quality of simultaneously being consistent with their broader history and discordant with the reality they'd shaped for themselves over the preceding decade. It wasn't just that their success had made the idea of sending a fake Fleetwood Mac on the road even more unthinkable than it had been in the early-1970s, but for the public at large the band was synonymous with five specific people. The special and sometimes-volatile chemistry and intertwined dramas of those five musicians made Fleetwood Mac seem like a unique personality rather than just a commercial proposition: even at their most ubiquitous.

After Buckingham left, the Fleetwood Mac brand name began to take precedence over the actual people in the band. This held true even when those five started performing together again in the 1990s. But in the moment of Buckingham's departure, Fleetwood, Nicks and the two McVies' decision to push forward with the tour was thoroughly sensible. In a 1988 interview, Nicks insisted: 'Lindsey left. So did that mean we were done? No. Why should the rest of us quit because of him?' In later years, Nicks expressed some misgivings that she didn't leave the band when Buckingham did, but in 1987, her staying made sense. In addition to expanding the sphere of independence from her former partner, touring behind the band's best-selling album in years, offered obvious material incentives. Pride played a part as well. Having to back out of the already-scheduled tour dates would've looked bad for the group.

Mick Fleetwood quickly recruited two singer-guitarists, who were announced as permanent members at a press conference less than two weeks later. Billy Burnette – already in the band's orbit thanks to his involvement in Mick Fleetwood's Zoo – was an obvious choice. But Mick recognized the group also needed someone to play lead guitar: which wasn't Burnette's forte. Pennsylvania-born Rick Vito started playing professionally in 1971, but hadn't recorded an album of his own yet. But prior to joining Fleetwood Mac, he *had* recorded with a host of well-known artists, including Todd Rundgren, Bonnie Raitt, and fittingly – considering his new gig – John Mayall, appearing on two of Mayall's 1970s records: *Notice To Appear* and *A Banquet In Blues.*

Christine McVie saw the new members as a means to reconnect with the group's roots: 'I don't want to say (Rick is) like Peter Green, but he plays wonderful blues *à la* Peter.' Despite the acclaim from his new bandmate, Vito approached his new gig with great humility, saying shortly after joining: 'This chance, it wasn't something I would've sat down and thought about being in my future.'

Mick – whose enthusiasm for playing live had been equal to, if not greater than, his desire to record another Fleetwood Mac album – also felt a renewed energy in the band. He compared this more-committed approach with the abbreviated *Mirage* tour several years earlier:

It felt good to be playing again, and the songs came together rather fast. Before our last tour, a lot of time was spent cogitating, then we'd creep up onstage and play a bit. Now we seem much more focused, there are no distractions, and the onus is on the band vs. the individual. I'm all for solo projects, but when they create these long time lapses, everyone gets jittery.

His concerns about solo albums notwithstanding, in many respects, the group members' solo projects shaped the lineup that went onstage for the Shake The Cage tour. Beyond the obvious impact of Buckingham's absence, the band added percussionist Okyerema Asante (who Fleetwood had met while recording *The Visitor* in Ghana, and who had recently performed with Paul Simon) and a trio of backing singers: Sharon Celani, Lori Perry and Elisecia Wright from Stevie Nicks' solo tour.

Nicks' solo work also influenced the setlist: now including 'Stand Back' and 'Has Anyone Ever Written Anything For You?' Fortunately, the prevalence of hits sung by Christine McVie and a selection of Peter Green-era numbers spotlighting Burnette and Vito, ensured the show wasn't just an extension of Nicks' solo tour from the year before. While most of the standard Buckingham songs (except for 'Go Your Own Way') were absent from the setlist, the band revisited two songs associated with him: 'World Turning,' and the *Buckingham Nicks* standout 'Don't Let Me Down Again.'

The tour – which opened at the Kemper Arena in Kansas City, Missouri on 30 September 1987 – was documented in a concert video also called

Tango In The Night, released the following year. Directed by the award-winning Wayne Isham (with additional material shot by Marty Callner), who oversaw Nicks' *Rock A Little* tour video, the release was filmed over two nights in December 1987 at San Francisco venue The Cow Palace. It's a fairly standard concert film, but succeeds in showing that audiences got their money's worth. McVie was in especially good voice, as was Nicks, though the latter seemed less assured in sections where her voice needed to blend with the other vocalists. Burnette and Vito didn't have quite the same intensity as Buckingham, but nevertheless looked and sounded like they belonged there. Underpinning it all was the tandem of John McVie and Mick Fleetwood, with Mick clearly feeling at home in the thick of it.

The first part of the tour concluded in Seattle shortly before Christmas. Shows by The Zoo – including a New Year's Eve 1987 performance featuring Stevie Nicks – kept some members busy. The band as a whole prepared to perform overseas early in the new year, for the first time since 1980. Unfortunately, Nicks contracted the Epstein-Barr virus, requiring shows in Australia to be canceled and other dates rescheduled. The tour's European leg started on 10 May 1988 in Edinburgh, followed by shows in Birmingham and London. From there, the band made their way to Sweden, Germany, the Netherlands and Ireland, with a few more UK shows for good measure, including the tour's final performance at the Manchester City Football Ground.

Shortly before the concerts in Europe, Mick Fleetwood married Sara Recor on 24 April 1988, after a suitably-rocky period in their relationship. John McVie – now a US citizen and in better health after an alcohol-induced seizure prompted him to stop drinking – served as the best man. In addition to the band, guests included various musicians and actors, and even Lindsey Buckingham.

Buckingham – who'd worked with his musical idol Brian Wilson and aspiring British band The Dream Academy since leaving Fleetwood Mac – was thanked by the band on their next release: one that found them taking stock of recent history, while starting to shape their future. Rather than start work on a new album immediately, the band opted to release a greatest-hits collection in November 1988. The track list varied between the United States and other countries – the latter including the UK hit 'Oh Diane'. But both editions included a pair of new songs. This pleased Rick Vito, who observed, 'It makes it easier to play on two tracks instead of ten. After all, we're going to be on an album which is probably going to be pretty successful.' The *Greatest Hits* album *was* successful, peaking at 14 in the US, 3 in the UK, and selling millions worldwide. Incorporating new songs into a greatest-hits release had become commonplace in the 1980s, but Fleetwood Mac had gotten ahead of that curve several years earlier by including new material on their 1980 live album.

As on that greatest-hits-by-default release, the two new songs on their official *Greatest Hits* collection were true-to-form for their respective writers, but failed to make much of an impression on the charts. 'As Long As You Follow' offered vintage McVie lines like 'I can live today if you give me tomorrow,' a pleasant melody, and a guitar solo that Rick Vito identified in a 1999 online Q&A session as his favorite from his time with the band. However, those efforts went largely under the radar. Despite strong performances on the Adult Contemporary and Mainstream Rock charts in the US, the single just missed the main Top 40 in the US and the UK.

While many – including Stevie Nicks – highlighted Christine McVie's stature as the band's hit songwriter, Nicks' new contribution to the *Greatest Hits* collection – 'No Questions Asked' – could've been a superior single. The band initially planned to include 'Paper Doll' – a song Nicks worked on with Rick Vito and his friend John Heron – but Mick decided he wasn't keen on the track, and 'No Questions Asked' took its place. Her strongest Fleetwood Mac song since 'Gypsy,' it distinguished itself from much of her recent solo work by feeling lived in and tangible.

> So how can you say
> Well I don't know what love is
> You haven't and you have no time for it
> You feel completely indifferent
> You feel pushed up against the wall
> And then one day it just almost goes away
> You spend lots of time alone
> Sometimes you spend years
> And you miss those arms that used to go around you

Though the Klonopin addiction was starting to affect Nicks' ability to work on music, she began recording her next solo album later in the year. In keeping with the pattern established in 1981, she once again found her music intertwined with her personal life.

1989: Every Time That You Walk In The Room

While friction in her working relationship with Lindsey Buckingham had been a significant factor in Stevie Nicks prioritizing her solo career, Buckingham's exit from Fleetwood Mac still left a major reason in place for her. The addition of Billy Burnette and Rick Vito meant the band now had four songwriters. Since the new lineup hadn't changed the frequency of band recording, Nicks still needed solo albums as an outlet for her songs. She recalled in 2007: 'Lucky me. I had written the songs for *The Other Side of the Mirror* before the Klonopin kicked in. I was very happy with them, and still am. I really love that record.'

To articulate these songs in the studio, she worked with British producer Rupert Hine, recording first at her home (or a Dutch castle, depending on which account you believe) in late 1988, then flying to the UK early in the new year to finish the album at his studio. During this time, the two briefly became romantically involved until – as Nicks recounted in 1991 – 'Something happened to him that simply made it impossible for us to ever be together again.'

Hine – who passed away in 2020 – started his music career in the 1960s as part of a folk duo called Rupert & David, before recording an album under his own name in 1971. When success as a performer eluded him, record production provided his path forward, starting with the curious *Doctor Who*-related single 'Who Is the Doctor?' by the program's star Jon Pertwee. In the 1980s, Hine produced albums for British artists Chris DeBurgh, Howard Jones, and also Tina Turner's US hit 'Better Be Good To Me.' The latter track featured guitarist Jamie West-Oram from British band The Fixx: a group Hine produced four albums for.

Guitar played a more prominent role on *The Other Side of the Mirror* than on *Rock a Little*. Along with Jamie West-Oram, Mike Campbell and Waddy Wachtel played on multiple tracks – in Wachtel's case, three times as many as the previous album. Campbell also co-wrote three songs, as did Rupert Hine. But in spite of the talented musicians involved, the end result was Stevie Nicks' most bland solo record to date. The technological artifice is less apparent, but like its predecessor, the album still feels constructed rather than crafted as *Bella Donna* or even *The Wild Heart* did.

Critics held more-favorable views, at least in the UK. *Record Mirror* reviewer Steve Masters rated *The Other Side of the Mirror* 4.5 out of 5 stars, praising Nicks as 'a musical Casanova, seducing even the most brazen ears.' Caveats about the 'overworked Alice-In-

Wonderland imagery' aside, *Music Week*'s Duncan Holland was similarly complimentary, calling the album 'a remarkably strong record.' In contrast, *Rolling Stone* writer Jimmy Guterman gave it a decidedly mixed review, writing, 'Nicks can stand tall with the top rank of contemporary rockers, but she's not nearly consistent enough to sustain a whole album. The *Chicago Tribune*'s David Silverman dismissed the album as 'A disappointing soundalike with no new ground broken.' Silverman's view was accurate on balance, but as with Nicks' other solo albums, that view was somewhat beside the point for the singer's fans. *The Other Side of the Mirror* returned Stevie Nicks to the US top ten, and became her first top ten album in the UK, where it was certified platinum and gold, respectively.

The Other Side of the Mirror – Stevie Nicks (1989)

Personnel:

Side One:

1. 'Rooms On Fire' (Nicks, Rick Nowels)
Stevie Nicks: lead vocals, percussion, Sharon Celani, Lori Perry-Nicks: backing vocals, Geoff Dugmore: drums, Vail Johnson: bass, Jamie West-Oram, Rick Nowels: guitar, Rupert Hine: keyboards, percussion

2. 'Long Way To Go' (Nicks, Nowels, Charles Judge)
Stevie Nicks: lead vocals, tambourine, Sharon Celani, Lori Perry-Nicks: backing vocals
Jerry Marotta: drums, Tony Levin: stick, Jamie West-Oram, Rick Nowels: guitar, Rupert Hine: keyboards

3. 'Two Kinds Of Love' (Nicks, Rupert Hine, Nowels)
Stevie Nicks: lead vocals, Bruce Hornsby: vocals, Sharon Celani, Lori Perry-Nicks: backing vocals
Rupert Hine: keyboards, programmed drums, percussion, Tony Levin: bass, Waddy Wachtel: acoustic guitar, Kenny G: soprano saxophone

4. 'Ooh My Love' (Nicks, Nowels)
Stevie Nicks: lead vocals, Lori Perry-Nicks: backing vocals, Jerry Marotta: drums, Vail Johnson: bass, Jamie West-Oram, Rick Nowels: guitar, Rupert Hine: keyboards, additional percussion

5. 'Ghosts' (Nicks, Mike Campbell)
Stevie Nicks: lead vocals, tambourine, Sharon Celani, Lori Perry-Nicks: backing vocals, Jerry Marotta: drums, Vail Johnson: bass, Mike Campbell: guitar, Rupert Hine: keyboards

6. 'Whole Lotta Trouble' (Nicks, Campbell)

Stevie Nicks: lead vocals, percussion, Sharon Celani, Lori Perry-Nicks:
backing vocals, Jerry Marotta: drums, Tony Levin: stick, Mike Campbell:
guitar, slide acoustic guitar, Waddy Wachtel, Jamie West-Oram: guitar,
Rupert Hine: keyboards, percussion, The L.A Horns – Jerry Hey, Gary Grant,
Mark Russo, Larry Williams: brass
Side Two:
1. 'Fire Burning' (Nicks, Campbell, Hine)
Stevie Nicks: lead vocals, tambourine, Sharon Celani, Lori Perry-Nicks:
backing vocals, Jerry Marotta: drums, Vail Johnson, Derek Murphy: bass, Mike
Campbell, Waddy Wachtel: guitar, Rupert Hine: keyboards
2. 'Cry Wolf' (Jude Johnstone)
Stevie Nicks: lead vocals, Sharon Celani, Lori Perry-Nicks: backing vocals,
Geoff Dugmore: dorms, keyboards, Tony Levin: bass, Jamie West-Oram:
guitar, Rupert Hine: keyboards
3. 'Alice' (Nicks, Hine)
Stevie Nicks: lead vocals, Sharon Celani, Lori Perry-Nicks: backing vocals,
Rupert Hine: keyboards, programmed drums, keyboard bass, Jamie West-
Oram, Waddy Wachtel: acoustic guitar, Kenny G: tenor sax
4. 'Juliet' (Nicks)
Stevie Nicks: lead vocals, tambourine, Sharon Celani, Lori Perry-Nicks:
backing vocals, Bruce Hornsby: additional vocals, piano, Jerry Marotta:
drums, Vail Johnson: bass, Waddy Wachtel: guitar, Mike Campbell: slide
acoustic guitar, Rupert Hine: keyboards
5. 'Doing The Best I Can (Escape From Berlin)' (Nicks)
Stevie Nicks: lead vocals, Sharon Celani, Lori Perry-Nicks: backing vocals,
Tony Levin: stick, Rupert Hine: keyboards, programmed drums, Jamie West-
Oram: guitar
6. 'I Still Miss Someone (Blue Eyes)' (Johnny Cash, Roy Cash Jr.)
Stevie Nicks: lead vocals, Sharon Celani, Lori Perry-Nicks: backing vocals,
Tony Levin: stick, Rupert Hine: keyboards, programmed drums, bass, Waddy
Wachtel: acoustic guitar, Kelly Johnston: whistle
Producer, arranger: Rupert Hine
Engineer, mixer: Stephen W. Tayler
Release date: 11 May 1989
Chart places: US: 10, UK: 3
Running Time: 56:10

The album's opening track and first single, 'Rooms On Fire', certainly
helped matters. Nicks' first solo hit in the UK, the single reached 16 there

and in the US, and displayed a sparkle missing from most of the album. In the liner notes for her 1991 compilation *Timespace*, she acknowledged Rupert Hine as an inspiration for the song, and subsequently related in a commentary for the song's music video, that 'This song was really about falling in love with somebody almost at first sight.' She also referred to it as being 'about the dream of having the long and beautiful relationship that doesn't get messed up.' Beyond the song's inspiration from her personal life, it's one of the album's few tracks where both the production style and the composition itself work to each other's advantage.

She had trusted many
And then there would be someone who would enter her presence
That she could sense for miles
She dreamed of her wanton luxury
And she laughed and she cried
And she tried to taunt him
And he hated to be separated
From that picture... no

After 'Rooms On Fire' set a high bar for the rest of the album, it isn't surprising that the tracks that immediately follow, disappoint. 'Long Way To Go' is energetic but unremarkable, with a tired lyric repeating sentiments Nicks has expressed much more artfully elsewhere.

It's a real long way to go to say goodbye
I thought we already did that
Have fun, tell the world

'Two Kinds Of Love' – co-written with Hine, and Nicks' *Rock a Little* collaborator Rick Nowels – is stranger still. Where the best of Stevie Nicks' solo work feels evergreen, this song, with vocals by Bruce Hornsby and a saxophone solo by Kenny G, feels time-stamped in the late-1980s. Like the preceding song, the lyric does this song no favours. The relatability that was one of Nicks' great strengths - even when her songs were at their most abstract and self-involved (sometimes simultaneously) – fades away when she foregrounds her star status.

Well I talked to my famous friend last night
My third day up, well, his second-nighter

He says, 'I don't know how you do what you do, How do you let the world in?'

Originally worked on with Fleetwood Mac for *Tango In the Night*, 'Ooh My Love' is much stronger. If anything, the recording here is superior to the demo by Fleetwood Mac, whose synth-pop approach was a rare case of Lindsey Buckingham misjudging the production style needed for one of Nicks' songs. The castle imagery is a bit obvious, but nonetheless appropriate for Nicks.

Yes it was a strain on her
Watching her castles fall down
Oh, but there was a time when he called her 'Angel'
Where in the world did you come from?

Side one concludes with two of the album's three songs written with Mike Campbell: 'Ghosts' and 'Whole Lotta Trouble.' The former has a solid sense of drama, thanks to lines like 'To feel the empty spaces she's feeling/She depends on her music like a husband.'

Despite failing to chart in the US, 'Whole Lotta Trouble' earned Stevie Nicks her fourth Grammy nomination in the female category for Best Rock Vocal Performance. Nicks and Campbell worked on 'Whole Lotta Trouble' while she was traveling on The True Confessions Tour in Australia, and Campbell recorded an early version of it with her after the *Rock A Little* tour. In the *Timespace* liner notes for, Nicks thanked Campbell for being 'The only person in my whole life who has *ever* done one of my songs exactly as I had written it.' Whatever the merits of that recording, the album version simply plods along.

The third Campbell collaboration – with reflected input from Hine as well – begins side two. Musically reminiscent of UK pop band The Searchers, 'Fire Burning' reflects Campbell and Nicks' 1960s pop inspirations, giving the song its charm. At the same time, Nicks gives the piece a more-committed performance than clichéd lines like 'There is no fire burning/Just a soul crying,' merit.

Fire imagery is also on display in 'Cry Wolf.' Written by Jude Johnstone – better known for her later work recorded by country artists such as Johnny Cash and Trisha Yearwood – American pop singer Laura Branigan had recorded the song in 1987 toward the end of her pop-star moment. Johnstone herself recorded it in 2002. As on the previous song,

Nicks sounds vocally engaged, even as lines about crying wolf don't give her much to work with.

'Alice' aspires to the grandeur of *The Wild Heart*'s 'Beauty And The Beast,' but co-writer Rupert Hine's production and Kenny G on saxophone lack the impact of that earlier track. Nor does Nicks do much to make the song's notional inspiration feel personal the way she did with the Jean Cocteau film in 1983. Nicks' lyric acknowledges the metaphorical potential of Lewis Carroll's story, to comment on questions of self – something she doubtless would've considered during her experience at the Betty Ford Center – but it never gets below the surface.

Like Alice through the looking glass
She used to know who she was
Call out my name, call out my name
But I get no answer, she prays

Another song Nicks worked on with Fleetwood Mac for *Tango In The Night*, 'Juliet' benefits from Bruce Hornsby's vocal and instrumental contributions. Combined with guitarists Mike Campbell and Waddy Wachtel, it brings the track closer to the feel of *Bella Donna* or *The Wild Heart*, with a lyric evoking some images of past work.

Turn to the blue crystal mirror
Well, as always it is truthful
Oh, well you see it in the reflection of the real blue lamp
Well, tie the connection
Get some ribbons and some bows
Get back out on the road
But when they were good, they were really good
Really good stranger

Any song with a subtitle like that for 'Doing The Best That I Can (Escape From Berlin),' is going to invite questions. Some of the lyric invites the interpretation that it's another song reflecting Nicks' experience with rehab a few years earlier: along similar lines to 'Welcome To The Room... Sara.'

I was silent, I was locked away
But I covered my tears

Silent all day
It's out of my hands here

In my distress, well, I wanted someone to blame me
In my devastation, I wanted so to change
In my way, disaster was the only thing I could depend on

Whatever her inspirations, the end result is affecting, and *The Other Side of the Mirror* would've been better if this had been the closing track. Instead, it ends with a reggae-inflected cover of Johnny Cash's 'I Still Miss Someone.' However much one might enjoy recasting the standards of one genre into another, Nicks' love of country music – and the acumen for it displayed on previous records – made this a puzzling choice. It doesn't help that this rendition comes across as more languid than wistful, and more than a little artificial.

'I Still Miss Someone' was not among the album's songs that were played on the tour that followed in August. The concerts – which included Nicks' first solo shows in Europe – gave a good representation of her work, even if 'Juliet' was dropped from the setlist while 'Two Kinds Of Love' and 'Whole Lotta Trouble' remained. Unfortunately – as Nicks explained in 2007 – 'Somewhere out on that tour, the (Klonopin) kicked in and brought me to my knees.' She described the multi-year period under the drug's influence as being 'worse than the cocaine years, because at least during those years I did something that I considered valuable.'

Though Stevie Nicks was the only Fleetwood Mac member to release music in 1989, she wasn't the only one in the public eye. Mick Fleetwood – taking a page from his sister Susan, whose acting roles ranged from *Clash of the Titans* to *The Buddha of Suburbia* – took up acting in the 1980s, making his debut in the 1987 movie *The Running Man*. In 1989, Mick appeared in *Star Trek: The Next Generation* and the acclaimed TV crime drama *Wiseguy*. At the time, *Wiseguy* was one of the few American non-soap-opera prime-time dramas that featured serialized storylines, and for one storyline involving the music business, the producers also cast fellow rock stars Glenn Frey and Debbie Harry.

Mick Fleetwood also reunited briefly with his old bandmate Peter Bardens for some shows in the United Kingdom. However, what surely made the drummer the happiest, was Fleetwood Mac's six-piece lineup returning to the studio before the end of the year, to record their next album. Despite debuting at number one in the UK, 1990's *Behind the Mask* was only a modest success relative to *Tango In The Night*. But having a solid new album and following it with a lengthy world tour just three years after the previous outing, probably felt like the next steps on a clear path forward: at least for Fleetwood.

But this period of relative stability was short-lived, and within a few years, a fresh set of tensions emerged. While the group's foundation – namely Mick Fleetwood and John McVie – were at the time largely untouched by these cracks, the long-term effects reshaped the band's membership and its legacy in suitably dramatic and unpredictable ways.

Epilogue: Time Casts A Spell

It's in the nature of iconic moments to stand out in the memory, even at the expense of the larger story. The *Rumours* lineup reuniting to perform 'Don't Stop' at President Bill Clinton's January 1993 inauguration was just such a moment. There's a temptation to draw a line from that rough-but-spirited stand-alone performance to the more substantial reunion that coalesced in 1997, but things are rarely so straightforward with Fleetwood Mac. Without diminishing the event's significance, it should also be acknowledged as an anomaly, falling squarely between two albums featuring materially different iterations of the band, and taking place less than two weeks before yet another lineup played at the Super Bowl pregame show.

President Clinton's inauguration wasn't even the first time Lindsey Buckingham had performed with the other four since leaving the band. Having played acoustic guitar on the title track of *Behind the Mask*, he also joined the band for a few songs at the final shows of their 1990 tour. Not long after that, Buckingham added vocals and guitar to Stevie Nicks' 'Paper Doll,' for inclusion on the 1992 retrospective *25 Years: The Chain*. The box set – which also featured new Christine McVie songs and one by Buckingham himself – sparked another internal feud: this one over a song from 15 years earlier. When selecting material for her first solo compilation, Stevie Nicks asked Mick Fleetwood about using the beloved *Rumours* outtake 'Silver Springs.' Since its previous release had been limited to the B-side of 'Go Your Own Way,' Mick refused, preferring the song's first album release to be in the Fleetwood Mac set. This revived the anger Nicks (who'd gifted the song's publishing rights to her mother) felt when the song was left off *Rumours*.

Stevie Nicks and Christine McVie announced their intention to stop touring with Fleetwood Mac in fall 1990 – shortly before the end of the tour for *Behind the Mask* – but left open the possibility of recording with the group in the future. The dispute with Fleetwood over 'Silver Springs,' changed Nicks' mind. She told the *Boston Globe* in 1991: 'I said, 'If you don't give me back my song, then I won't write two new songs for your new record.' I never burn bridges, but right now, I don't think I'll work with them.'

Nicks' frustration with Mick Fleetwood aside, she was apparently the one who convinced a reluctant Lindsey Buckingham to participate in the inauguration performance. Nevertheless, the band's 1995 album *Time* became their first in two decades not to include Nicks, and was their worst seller in many years. With Rick Vito also having left after *Behind The Mask*, and Christine McVie making only limited studio contributions, Mick Fleetwood once again drew from The Zoo – recruiting Bekka Bramlett: daughter of Eric Clapton associates Delaney and Bonnie Bramlett. Mick's longtime friend – former Traffic member Dave Mason – completed the lineup, but the new iteration barely registered with fans.

Time sold poorly, and the band's 1995 shows in the US were part of a package tour with Pat Benatar and REO Speedwagon: two successful acts whose heyday had passed. Fleetwood wrote in 2014: 'We should never have done any of it. We were a totally different band, with only the original drummer and bass player, and our original name. Had Christine remained, there would've been three of us, and that would've been defensible.'

One of the more thoughtful defenses of Fleetwood Mac's 1995 iteration actually came from Lindsey Buckingham. Despite his disappointment at the band becoming a nostalgia act, he expressed empathy for Fleetwood when discussing the period in a 1997 *Mojo* article:

> The very thing Mick did after Peter Green – this constant process of opening the band to various incarnations, a lot of which were kind of non sequiturs – that was the very process that led him to us. And I think in his mind, he was just doing the same thing he always did. And maybe the difference is, that after a big success, that idea doesn't work so well.

Success was elusive for all the band members in the mid-1990s. Stevie Nicks' 1994 solo album *Street Angel* – recorded prior to her going into rehab to address the Klonopin addiction – sold poorly. So did Lindsey Buckingham's 1992 masterpiece *Out of the Cradle*, despite glowing reviews. When Nicks approached Buckingham about him producing and playing on 'Twisted' – a track for the 1996 movie *Twister* – he was already working on his fourth solo album, with some help from Mick Fleetwood and both John and Christine McVie.

In an echo of the 1980s, the overlapping projects led to Buckingham putting the mostly-completed record aside in favor of a more-substantial Fleetwood Mac reunion. Recorded for MTV in spring 1997, *The Dance* was memorialized in a live album of the same name, which became Fleetwood Mac's first number-1 US album since *Mirage*, and paved the way for a much more popular US tour than the band's 1995 iteration had experienced.

Beyond its scope, the 1997 reunion also reflected a change in the attitudes and dynamics between the group members. Mick Fleetwood revealed in a 1997 article in *Goldmine*: 'I've gotten real close to Lindsey over the last year, to a place we've never been before.' Later that year, in a piece for *The Houston Press*, Stevie Nicks explained how their 1993 gathering changed her feelings about the band: '(The inauguration) made me realize that it had to be that five, or it couldn't be. I couldn't continue to be in a Fleetwood Mac that didn't have Lindsey in it.'

Coming three years after The Eagles' reunion and their bestselling collection of live hits and new material *Hell Freezes Over*, *The Dance* inevitably drew comparisons with it, *and* suggestions that money played a bigger role than music. 'It'll be surprising if someone doesn't think that,' said John McVie in *Mojo*. In the same piece, Buckingham drew a sharp contrast between Fleetwood Mac and their similarly-fractious contemporaries: 'In the same way, maybe people *can* sense that Don and Glenn maybe aren't that crazy about being onstage with each other, they can sense that we *are* really digging it.'

The presence of 'Silver Springs' on *The Dance* – among standards like 'Say You Love Me' and 'The Chain' – also reflected diminished conflict within the group. It allowed Nicks and Buckingham to acknowledge the past without any apparent acrimony, and the financial benefit her mother received from the song's inclusion on a bestselling album, likely smoothed over any lingering resentment about Mick Fleetwood not allowing her to use the song on *Timespace*. The live rendition was nominated at the 1998 Grammy Awards, along with the album itself – the group's first Grammy nominations since *Rumours* won the award for Album of the Year at the 1978 ceremony.

As with that period two decades earlier, the sensible choice would've been to retire on top after their victory lap, especially after Christine McVie decided to leave the band and return to England following the band's induction into the Rock and Roll Hall of Fame. However, because the history of Fleetwood Mac is a story of unhealthy patterns being repeated, further collaboration and further conflict was inevitable. Aside from a performance at a farewell party for President Clinton as he prepared to leave office in January 2001, the band remained dormant for a couple years after McVie's departure.

Having helped reinvigorate Fleetwood Mac, Stevie Nicks did the same for her solo work. The Klonopin addiction derailed her songwriting, but her struggle to re-engage was rewarded when her 2001 album *Trouble In*

Shangri-La reached the top 5 in the United States, around the same time Destiny's Child used a sample of 'Edge Of Seventeen' in their hit single 'Bootylicious.' Along with artists who'd been influenced by Nicks – such as Sheryl Crow and Sarah McLachlan – *Trouble In Shangri-La* featured longtime musical associates like Waddy Wachtel, Benmont Tench and even Lindsey Buckingham. For his part, Buckingham found the record company more interested in his recently-completed solo album after it became his second to morph into a Fleetwood Mac project.

Though the other four hoped she might join them, Christine McVie's role on the album was limited to some keyboards and backing vocals on two songs, recorded when they were still meant for Buckingham's album. Despite this, the magazine *Classic Rock* declared 2003's *Say You Will* as Fleetwood Mac's 'first studio record since 1987 that really matters.' With nine songs each from Buckingham and Nicks, *Say You Will* sometimes felt more like solo albums from each singer played on shuffle than the long-delayed follow-up to *Tango In The Night*. Still, songs like 'What's The World Coming To?,' 'Thrown Down' and 'Illume' (the latter inspired by Nicks' experiences being in New York City during the 9/11 terrorist attacks) showed the band pushing themselves to a degree well beyond expectations.

Both the album and the tour that followed were successful, but had little long-term impact for the band. Only two of the album's songs were played live after the tour ended in 2004, and the setlist for their next one in 2009 put the emphasis firmly on their 1975-1987 prime. By this time, it became apparent that – in contrast with 1987 – this time it was Nicks rather than Buckingham acting out of obligation to the band, against her better judgment. In spite of her previous comments about not wanting to be in the band without Lindsey Buckingham, or praising *Say You Will* in 2003 as 'that great thing he always wanted to do,' Christine McVie seemed to be the one Nicks missed the most. Nicks told *Performing Songwriter* in 2007: 'It was a nightmare doing that record' – a condition she directly attributed to making the album without McVie. 'She is the magic mediator in that band, and always was. She's the one who made light of everything and made everybody laugh and told us all we were full of shit.' In the same interview, Nicks dismissed the idea of making another Fleetwood Mac album without Christine McVie. Though, it turned out she wasn't especially interested in doing one *with* her either.

When Christine McVie rejoined Fleetwood Mac in 2014 after guest appearances at shows in London the year before, questions about the possibility of a new album by the classic lineup, followed. McVie and Buckingham soon started working on songs together, with John McVie and Mick Fleetwood on bass and drums, but Stevie Nicks opted to not participate. Had they released the material as a Fleetwood Mac album, it would've had a strong claim for being the band's best record since *Tango In The Night*. Instead, the Buckingham and McVie put the album out under their own names in 2017, accompanied by a joint tour mixing their own work and Fleetwood Mac songs.

The band's latest period of relative calm came to an end early in 2018 when Buckingham received a phone call from manager Irving Azoff. Azoff – who now managed the band as a whole rather than just Stevie NIcks – relayed a message from her to the effect that she never wanted to be on stage with Lindsey again. In light of her ultimatum to the rest of the band that either he go or she would leave, Buckingham became one of the few people to actually be fired from Fleetwood Mac, and sued his former bandmates.

True to form, the reasons for this development are a matter of dispute, and largely irrelevant. In April 2018, Fleetwood Mac announced a new lineup that featured Mike Campbell from Tom Petty and the Heartbreakers, and Crowded House leader Neil Finn, in advance of a tour later in the year. While Buckingham's mid-1980s comments comparing Christine McVie and Stevie Nicks' solo performances to a lounge act because of their inclusion of band material were uncharitable and ironic, considering the setlist of his own shows, this version of the group suggested he wasn't necessarily wrong. Campbell's long association with Nicks notwithstanding, both he and Finn seemed chosen more on the basis of attracting fans of their previous groups than any particular affinity with Fleetwood Mac.

A year after his removal from the band, Buckingham faced a more-grievous challenge when his vocal cords were damaged during medical treatment following a heart attack. This was indicative of a difficult decade for Fleetwood Mac guitarists, ranging from the 2012 suicide of Bob Welch to the more-peaceful 2020 passing of Peter Green, and also the deaths of Danny Kirwan, Bob Weston and original bassist Bob Brunning. Buckingham recovered and released his seventh solo album in September 2021, a few months after his wife, Kristen Messner, filed for divorce. The self-titled record's release was accompanied by multiple interviews offering his particular take on the events surrounding his dismissal. Those comments provoked expectedly-contrary responses from both Stevie Nicks and Irving Azoff, though the improbability of Buckingham reconnecting with the group for a farewell tour has as much to do with the other members.

Fleetwood Mac played their last show to date in November 2019, and any longer-term plans they had were sidelined by the COVID-19 pandemic. In 2021, Christine McVie told a BBC radio interviewer that she didn't expect either Stevie Nicks or John McVie to take part in any future Fleetwood Mac shows, and wondered if she might also be too old for it herself. The one member whose commitment Mcvie was sure of, was Mick Fleetwood, who she said 'would do it in a lightning strike.'

McVie's observation dovetailed with Fleetwood's self-deprecating comment from three decades earlier: 'I'm going to be an 80-year-old rocker, and they'll have to take me out and shoot me to get me to stop.' Sadly, the announcement of Christine McVie's sudden passing on 30 November 2022 means another, more idealistic goal the drummer had won't come to pass. As he described to *Rolling Stone* in 2021: 'Somehow, I would love the elements that are not healed, to be healed. I love the fantasy that we could cross that bridge and everyone could leave with creative, holistic energy, and everyone could be healed with grace and dignity."

Above: The momentum from *Tango in the Night's* success helped the band's new line-up get off to a strong start.

Right: While commercially successful, *The Other Side of the Mirror* was Stevie Nicks' blandest solo album to date.

Left: Recorded with Fleetwood Mac's new line-up, *Behind the Mask* was a good record but suffered from comparison with its predecessors. (*Warner Bros.*)